*MYTH*MANAGEMENT

To Susan, Lora and J. R.

*MYTH*MANAGEMENT

An Examination of Corporate Diversification as Fact and Theory

Milton Leontiades

Basil Blackwell

Copyright © Milton Leontiades, 1989

First Published 1989

Basil Blackwell Ltd
108 Cowley Road, Oxford, OX4 IJF, UK

Basil Blackwell Inc.
3 Cambridge Center
Cambridge, Massachusetts 02142, USA

British Library Cataloguing in Publication Data
A CIP catalogue record for this book is available from the British Library.

Library of Congress Cataloging in Publication Data

Leontiades, Milton.
    Mythmanagement : an examination of corporate diversification as
fact and theory / Milton Leontiades.
      p. cm.
    Includes index.
    ISBN 0–631–15931–2
    1. Diversification in industry. 2. Industrial management.
    3. Business education. I. Title. II. Title: Myth management.
    HD2756.L465   1989   89–33262
    658.5′038–dc20   CIP

Typeset in 10 on 12 point Times
by Vera-Reyes Inc., Philippines
Printed in Great Britain by Billing and Sons Ltd., Worcester

Contents

Preface

What began as a book about corporate diversification extended into a discussion of economics and business education. Once I began the research, it became obvious that a single theme on diversification would not suffice. Standing in the way is an existing theoretical structure that perceives diversification as noncompetitive in all but a very narrow sense. The rationale for such a stance has its roots in economic theory, some of which dates back more than two hundred years. Yet economic theory of how firms compete – the so-called theory of the firm – is outlandishly at odds with what businesses do, as economists readily admit. This conundrum brought me to the question of business education, which in several respects seems bent on imitating the position of economics. Why would business schools pick up the ancient myths of economics? And does the educational system somehow encourage the perpetuation of myths over the creation of better theory? In addressing these questions, I made a temporary detour from my main topic of diversification; however, no significant progress can be made towards new concepts of diversification without first clearing away the accumulated myths that support the conventional wisdom and impede new ideas from emerging.

Also, I wanted to reach both an academic and a business readership. If progress is to be made towards bringing theory and practice together, both parties will have to contribute to a resolution. Yet communicating in a language acceptable, and understandable, to both sides is difficult. Practical business books that typically sell well offer one-minute "bites" of knowledge, easily digestible and promptly forgotten. On the other hand, the most elevated scholarly works generally reach the smallest audiences and are inaccessible to the average reader. Trying to find a middle ground, I have attempted to document my position meticulously in the first two chapters with reference to supporting opinions of recognized authorities, and have relied upon examples reflecting real business practices and managerial decision-making in the last two chapters. I am aware that this method risks satisfying neither side completely, but I feel that an effort to communicate bilaterally is absolutely essential. Without input from business experience, higher education's teaching about business rings hollow. And without a coherent framework for explaining businesses' actions, business education is reduced to anecdotal incidents and storytelling. Even a small aid in joining more closely these two parties with a vested interest in the quality of business education would justify the effort. Getting both academics and business people simply to engage actively in a discussion of the issues would in itself signify a milestone of progress.

Because diversification cuts across a range of interests, including a variety of views and approaches, it is impossible to do justice to the full scope of the subject. Some of the economics studies, in particular, are very technical in nature and for the sake of readability are either excluded or dealt with in plain English.

Finally, the focus of the book is on American business firms. Although this limitation is necessary in order to cover what I know best, I believe that the book's main thesis is applicable to other industrialized nations, with especially close reference to Japan and the major European trading partners with the United States.

As a postscript, I would like to absolve all colleagues and friends from guilt in encouraging me to take on what at times seemed an endless and impossible assignment.

Introduction

As a student, I felt my training in business and economics gave me a good idea of how business worked. After graduation, and several job experiences, I found that what I had learned and what I needed to know were considerably at odds. Going back to school for a postgraduate degree, while still working, reaffirmed my first impressions. In particular, in economics, the subject of my doctorate, the distance between what was being taught and what I knew from experience was so, represented an almost unbridgeable gap. At the time, I was working as an economist in the Office of Fiscal Analysis of the United States Treasury Department. Thus, I was ostensibly well informed on fiscal affairs. Yet on a five-part written examination in review of course work taken toward the PhD degree, I scored lowest on the part dealing with fiscal policy, the area where my working knowledge would presumably have prepared me the best. It was as if the more I knew, the less it mattered.

The wide gap between theory and fact bothered me off and on for many years. Eventually, I left the private sector and became a professor in a large state university. From the inside, I reasoned, my business background would help me, in a small way, move business and theory closer together. What I discovered is an academic system remarkably detached from professional contact with the business community: faculty members and administrators are essentially free to shape the academic curriculum to suit their needs. Apparently satisfied with the status quo, both faculty members and administrators of the top business schools – those generally designated by their strong research orientation – appear committed to a standard of excellence that is both self-defined and self-serving. Within this insulated environment business schools are on the way to creating myths of management: theories on how business should work or might work that do not depend on knowledge of actual business firms or motivations of real business managers. By constructing hypothetical models remote from experience and remaining faithful to them, business educators attain the supreme intellectual achievement of logical perfection, protected from the intrusion of contradictory factual evidence.

What might happen to business has already happened in economics, where faculty members address themselves to their colleagues and their discipline in a highly technical and specialized language that excludes a larger general public. Like business, economics began as the study of policy issues by persons knowledgeable in practical affairs. Political economy, as economics was initially known, implied an intimacy with the workings of the economic system in order to recommend how best to improve prevailing economic conditions. Eventually, however, science crowded out policy as the main thrust of economics, and mathematical formulae became the preferred means for analyzing and portraying economic ideas. As a consequence, the study of economics became frozen in time. Static equilibrium, a precondition for rigorous mathematical analysis, became part of the internal structure in modern economic theorizing.

For a while, economists had deliberated between choosing the economics of change, exemplified perhaps best by Joseph Schumpeter's concept of "creative destruction" and its underlying presumption that dynamic disequilibrium was the normal condition, or the economics of static equilibrium and stability. Ultimately, the latter was chosen, not because it accorded with the facts, but because it lent itself to the scientific tools of mathematical economics. Once the profession had made its decision to mold itself into a science modeled on the physical sciences, economics had little choice but to emphasize stability over change, and the building of abstract economic models rather than the study of policy matters.

Business education is not yet at its own point of having to choose between science and practice, but evidence suggests a leaning toward development of a "science" of management. Business-school curricula currently reflect the recommendations contained in the 1959 Ford- and Carnegie-sponsored studies on higher education in business.[1] Written by economists, these two studies bear the unmistakable imprint of the philosophy of economic science. An update on business education sponsored by the American Assembly of Collegiate Schools of Business (AACSB), nearly thirty years later, leans heavily on the logic developed in the Ford and Carnegie studies.[2] The AACSB report finds, however, that business people place significantly more emphasis on the value of applied research and nonquantitative aspects of a business education than do deans, faculty, and business-school alumni. Moreover, although abstract research in highly technical journals is the *sine qua non* for advancing the career of business educators, business men and women themselves typically ignore such research: "typically [business men and women] can safely ignore most business school research with impunity."[3] Despite the apparent disparity between business teachings and useful applications, the AACSB survey found "no forceful push for systematic curriculum change emanating from business schools themselves."[4]

Once removed from public accountability, it is relatively easy for academic myths of either the business or economic variety to flourish and, once accepted as part of the current orthodoxy, they become strongly resistant to pressures for change. Incorporated into textbooks, and perpetuated in teachings by new faculty members, myths tend to assume lives of their own, separate and apart from the actual phenomenon they supposedly address.

Adam Smith's theory of perfect competition is a classic example. Built on an assumption of miniature firms with miniscule market shares engaging each other in no-win competitive contests, Smith's version of competition bears no semblance to modern capitalism. Nor is it taken seriously as an accurate picture of competitive behavior by economists themselves. What it offers economists is an internally consistent model of competition that lends itself well to pedagogy, and scientific techniques of research. Adam Smith's theory of perfect competition lives on, in other words, not because it depicts competition, but because it is perfect. Although it does not accord with the facts, it is the best theory economists have to offer. As such, it will not be abandoned until a better-constructed theory is available, even in light of all the obvious factual discrepancies in the current version.

Because economics' past is potentially management's future, a considerable amount of attention is given to economics. Although this book is not about economics *per se,* the concern is that management will take the misguided tack of applying the scientific approach used in economic analysis as a valid approach to business problems.

Business is a practice. There are concrete reasons for business behavior that cannot be captured in a purely abstract method of reasoning. Removing real business firms from the study of business, as economics has done, is like studying medicine with no knowledge of human anatomy. In all the professions, there is an unavoidable mixture of art and science. Both have an important role to play and neither, by itself, can do justice to the complexities of real life. The clear danger for management, at this juncture, is to succumb to an intellectual temptation to gain peer recognition as the science of management – just as economics insists on describing itself as the science of economics.

Microeconomics, or the so-called theory of the firm, has not undergone appreciable change since Adam Smith set its foundations over two hundred years ago. In modern economics, the primary emphasis is on macroeconomics, or the economy in general. Business education, however, is principally concerned with activities within the firm. In the Ford- and Carnegie-sponsored studies of business education, a course in "business policy" was recommended as an opportunity to integrate the learning from separate business fields and to apply this knowledge toward the analysis of complex business problems. For the first time, the study of business was to be directed at the business firm itself. Subsequently, the business policy course has become the terminal or capstone course in the normal business-school curriculum.

Because the business policy course represents business education's equivalent of the theory of the firm, it provides a point of contrast between economics and business. In economics, the model of perfect competition defines how firms act. Although it is not realistic – a point economists concede – it is still faithfully reproduced in textbooks and taught in classrooms. In the business policy course, on the other hand, the students are expected to deal with real-life problem settings. Students generally assume the top manager's role. Using realistic business cases, students oversee a complex set of issues, analyze the situation, and develop strategies for action. The idea is to capture as closely as possible the essence of managing a real business, complete with the uncertainties and partial data that characterize real decision-making. The unstructured aspect of business cases makes the business policy course unsuitable for a strictly formulistic method of analysis. The emphasis in the business policy course is on the future – and on change. Business managers cannot be sure that, in an uncertain and unforeseeable future, decisions made currently will work out as planned. In practice, business managers must stand ready to adapt strategies to fit changes in forecasts. This requires a certain flexibility in decision-making: an openness to new thinking and new ideas as well as the willingness to abandon obsolete assumptions.

Yet what I see happening in the business policy course is a movement to freeze assumptions: to close debate around static notions of how businesses behave in order to get on with the compelling task of research and publication – the principal preoccupation of untenured business faculty members. By developing an internal consensus on hypotheses of how companies act, business scholars free themselves to concentrate on analytical techniques, while ignoring the external validity of their assumptions.

The tendency to favor technique over substance increasingly stretches management's credibility when it tries to reconcile theory with events. By diverting attention from what is to what their models say it is, management scholars, like economists before them, eventually will face a choice between fabricating reality and dealing with it directly. Whereas business policy is used to make this point in a general way, corporate diversification is the specific strategy of the firm employed in the book to provide a deeper investigation of this phenomenon.

How and why firms diversify occupies the second half of this book. The way companies solve the issue of diversification often makes the difference between corporate success and corporate failure. Of all the strategies managers must ponder, diversification is perhaps the most pressing for the modern business firm. Diversification deals with the fundamental issues of corporate evolution, growth, and ultimately survival of the firm itself. Progress thus far in developing a testable explanation of the diversification movement of business firms during the last three decades or so, however, is practically nil.

Borrowing extensively from economics, management scholars have developed an explanation of diversification that contains, in large measure, the deficiencies of economic methodology. Specifically, the notion of specialization, as developed in economics, serves as business education's basic rationale of how and why businesses evolve. Actions by managers and their expressed desire for growth, however, do not accord with specialization's logic. Strictly interpreted, specialization would limit companies to production of one product and commitment to a single industry. Even with liberalization, specialization as a concept cannot possibly explain the drive to diversify exemplified by modern business firms. Since the 1950s the move toward multi-product, multi-business organizations has evolved in direct contradiction to the economist's iron law of specialization.

Specialization as an explanation of corporate change does not fit the facts in the United States or in any foreign industrialized country. Japanese conglomerates have been especially succeful in defying the dictates of specialization. In the process, the Japanese have wrested market leadership away from their American competitors in industry after industry.

If the Japanese had subscribed to the common wisdom about specialization, they would still be trying to sell textiles and cheap radios to the United States. Instead, the Japanese broke away from conventional thinking and their past, and concentrated instead on an innovative strategy designed to create their future. Had Japanese companies stuck with what they did best, they would have remained in labor-intensive industries, where their comparative advantage *vis-à-vis* the United States was vast. Instead, they chose industries *least* appropriate from the vantage point of comparative advantage and specialization such as steel, automobiles, and industrial machinery, and later electronics and computers. From a static viewpoint, this strategy moved away from Japan's historic strengths and toward its weaknesses. But to Japanese officials, imperatives for change were clear: "If the Japanese economy had adopted the simple doctrine of free trade and had chosen to specialize in [one] kind of industry, it would have been unable to break away from the Asian pattern of stagnation and poverty."[5]

The enormous success enjoyed by Japanese companies can be attributed in part to a willingness to challenge accepted doctrines and beliefs. The perceived necessity to innovate overshadowed hypothetical arguments that argued against success. Japanese managers owe none of their enormous success to formal education or instruction. There were no business schools (as of the early 1980s). Japan's chief executives had read no books on competitive strategy, nor availed themselves of systematic analyses of how to plan. What, then, accounted for their incredible string of victories? The views of Kenichi Ohmae, Japan's best-known consultant on strategy and the managing director of McKinsey and Company's offices in Japan, are instructive on this point.

> [Japan's corporations have] a strategist of great natural talent: usually the founder or chief executive . . . they have an intuitive grasp of the basic elements of strategy. They have an idiosyncratic mode of thinking in which company, customers, and competition merge in a dynamic interaction out of which a comprehensive set of objectives and plans for action eventually crystallizes . . . the resulting plans might not even hold water from the analyst's point of view.[6]

In other words, Japanese managers rely on uniquely varied and heuristic reasoning processes, just the opposite from the exacting and inflexible model of perfect competition. Moreover, the competitive experiences of Japanese, European, and American companies do not remotely support the type of competition that pursuit of specialization alone would be expected to produce.

Thomas Huxley said once that tragedy in science "is the slaying of a beautiful hypothesis by an ugly fact." It is time to slay some of the "beautiful hypotheses" in higher business education that go disguised as science. There are many, many real-life business problems for business scholars and educators to address without contriving artificial solutions for mythical firms. In order to reunite theory with policy, however, there must be a willingness to sacrifice the status quo, to test constantly the assumptions of theory against the factual evidence. Business scholars must develop their own standards of excellence in scholarship. They must take an independent perspective, coordinating their outlook with other academic disciplines while, at the same time, avoiding domination by existing traditions and theories. Where conflicts arise, let the facts decide. Too often, the reaction now automatically is to defend a theory simply because it is the best available and to discredit or ignore contrary factual evidence.

The purpose of this book is to sound a caution for business schools. Put simply, business education needs to get back to the basics: a curriculum and research orientation centered on the business firm. Unlike economics, to which business is often compared and confused, the subject of business is business. All three sponsored reports on higher education in business by the Ford and Carnegie Foundations as well as the AACSB endorsed the applied aspect of business education: preparation of students for careers in business. This goal cannot be achieved satisfactorily while remaining detached from business policy-making, either in teaching or in research.

This book is not primarily prescriptive. It is not intended to give absolute answers, although some guidelines on redirection of management education are offered. It certainly is not intended as a rounded commentary on economic education, although considerable space is devoted to this academic discipline. Even on the specific question of diversification, the recommendations are meant to display insight rather than definitive conclusions. The intent is to ask the right questions, rather than develop sharp answers. Creating a philosophy of management is seen as being more important than specific techniques and tools of implementation. Where the greater fallacy lies currently is in advancing arguments wrapped so tightly in logic that they exclude all but a single and inflexible approach to the truth. Therein lies the prospect for creating myths that endure long after original circumstances have changed. Adam Smith, a lecturer on moral philosophy as well as economics, long ago cautioned:

> The improvements which, in modern times, have been made in several branches of philosophy, have not, the greater part of them, been made in universities; though some no doubt have. The greater part of universities have not even been very forward to adopt those improvements, after they were made; and several of those learned societies have chosen to remain, for a long time, the sanctuaries in which exploded systems and obsolete prejudices found shelter and protection, after they had been hunted out of every other corner of the world.[7]

This book is dedicated to avoiding such a predilection toward myopia in management education.

Notes

1 Robert A. Gordon and James Howell, *Higher Education for Business* (Columbia University Press, New York, 1959); Frank C. Pierson, *The Education of American Businessmen* (McGraw-Hill, New York, 1959).
2 Lyman W. Porter and Lawrence E. McKibbin, *Management Education and Development* (McGraw-Hill, New York, 1988).
3 Ibid., p. 304.
4 Ibid., p. 80.
5 Organization for Economic Co-operation and Development, *The Industrial Policy of Japan*, p. 15; as quoted in Thomas K. McCraw, *America versus Japan* (Harvard Business School Press, Boston, Mass., 1986), p. 9.
6 Kenichi Ohmae, *The Mind of the Strategist* (McGraw-Hill, New York, 1982), p. 2.
7 Adam Smith, *The Wealth of Nations*, Book V, as quoted in Walter Adams and James W. Brock, *The Bigness Complex* (Pantheon Books, New York, 1986), p. xiii.

1
Mythmanagement as Mythscience

Myths are stories. Like history, they speak of events, places, and things. Myths, however, are fictitious, whereas history is truthful, or at least intended to be factual. Thus, myths and historical fact are seldom confused. Princes, maidens in distress, knights, and castles obviously exist only in a fantasy land. There are, however, more subtle forms of myths where mythmaking is not deliberate, and the storyteller is not aware of the myth and believes that the account given is accurate. Moreover, when myths presume to be based on scientific study, the line between mythology and real life becomes hard to draw. One person's myth can be another's firmly and honestly held belief. Where the truth lies in these instances is not always easy to determine and can result in polarization, wherein two parties may lay claim to the truth when clearly only one can be right.

The myths that are of concern here are about business: how firms operate, compete, and change. The chief mythmakers are seen as economists. Their so-called "theory of the firm" – a micro-study of how resources are allocated – is the main myth. Although actual business firms are not an integral part of the economist's theory, economics purports to explain that sector of the economy in which firms operate. Moreover, despite its lack of descriptive power, the economist's theory of the firm is deemed to be scientifically grounded – a criterion for all economic theories in order to qualify them as part of the social "science" of economics. That is, any theory, including the theory of the firm, must contain an internally consistent logic that can be quantified and that gives precise and unqualified answers. The economist's approach, based as it is on the impression of accuracy from using scientific tools, has appeal for management scholars as well, a number of whom have emulated the methodology, along with the myths, that underlie economic theory.

My purpose here is to argue for moving the study of business closer to the reality of business. More precisely, it is to hold theory accountable: to measure the assumptions about firm behavior against observable and verifiable routines of business firms. A search for the truth, and the discarding of myths, clearly would serve the ends of the colleges and universities entrusted with the education of our future business leaders. Aligning research and teaching about business closer with the workings of business firms and the industries in which they operate could only improve the understanding of American enterprise and lead to better recommendations on improving its efficiency. Faculty members of business schools and business departments obviously have a stake in improving their understanding of business. Businesses also have vested interests in assuring that the scholarship *on* business has application *to* business.

This common-sense, even pedantic, message faces strong counter-pressures, however. Myths become real if they are accepted and assimilated into the unified culture of an academic environment. Once accepted, myths transform over time into general principles which, if allowed to become embedded, perpetuate within an academic system uniquely insulated from external review and criticism. Because university faculties control what is taught, and also who teaches, through the appointment, promotion, and tenuring process, reforming the system means challenging the current orthodoxy and converting the faithful.

I am, however, getting ahead of the story. An unflattering allusion to mythmaking in economics has been asserted, but not demonstrated. Deception in the form of myths has been implied, but not explained. In due course, both areas will be attended to. In addition, substitutes for traditional myththeory on the firm will be proposed, including a view of what drives firms to manage as they have, followed by proposals for change and improvement.

In this chapter, economics is used as the proxy to see where management might go, if beguiled by the neat logic of scientific method. Economics *per se* is not of direct concern; only its implication for the future of business education is examined here. In order to narrow the areas for discussion, economics and business are considered to be represented by the traditional modes described below.

Economics: A Working Definition

In general, references to economics and economists are aimed at the majority view: the mainstream of economic thought that emphasizes macroeconomics – the study of the overall economy – and uses mathematics and statistics as its principal analytical tools. Popular economics textbooks are the guides to what traditional economics still considers as a sound economic education. Although this perspective cannot do justice to all of economics or cover the many variations on the main theme, it captures the essence of economics in one key respect: the reliance on quantitative analysis.

Microeconomics – the behavior of individual units within the economy, such as firms, industries, and households – is of secondary interest to the economics mainstream, at least as measured by the amount of space occupied in economics textbooks, although it is the primary focus of business administration and of this book. The model of perfect competition, which underpins the economist's theory of the firm, is at the core of microeconomics. It assumes three attributes about firms: (1) standardized products (each firm's product is identical to that of its competitor's), (2) many small buyers and sellers (no single unit exerts influence on the market or market prices), and (3) freedom of entry and exit (new firms are free to enter, and old firms to leave, industries). Although perfect competition may be rare, it survives as the standard fare that students of economics are expected to learn and, implicitly, conveys the economist's norm for analyzing firm efficiency and competitiveness.

Business: A Working Definition

When discussing business or management, as the terms are interchangeably used, the orientation is toward general management. That is, the view is from the top and cuts across all the various functional activities – like accounting, marketing, organization, personnel, etc. – in order to concentrate on strategy and overall policy directives that control the firm as a whole. In most colleges and universities a final "capstone" course provides this overview, generally known as the course in business policy. Introduction of such a course into the business curriculum was prompted by the studies of higher education for business sponsored by the Ford Foundation, written by Gordon and Howell,[1] and the Carnegie Foundation, written by Frank Pierson.[2] These studies recognized the need for a required course that would present an integrated view of general management from the broad perspective of top management. The Ford Foundation study made the following recommendation:

> The capstone of the core curriculum should be a course in "business policy" which will give students an opportunity to pull together what they have learned in the separate business fields and utilize this knowledge in the analysis of complex business problems. The business policy course can offer the student something he will find nowhere else in the curriculum.

Prior to adoption of a business policy course, firms were typically viewed only in terms of their functional parts. Nowhere was the firm in its entirety studied. A completely new course and field of study was clearly needed, one that finally made room in business education for the study of business itself.

The Gap between Business Experience and Business Education

While I was employed in the private sector, I was convinced of the need for this type of reorientation. Being trained as an economist, I knew the shortcomings of the existing economic theory of the firm. Observing various businesses from the inside, I was aware that managements were preoccupied with the short term. Too little attention was being paid to why things were done or how they could be done better until firms were forced to change, either because of competitors' moves or other external threats. Detached studies of business lost priority to short-term problems and day-to-day details.

In the mid-1970s, I switched from a career in business to teaching business in higher education. A move from business to higher education had been planned long ago; the timing for a change seemed right. The new course in business policy offered an ideal area of concentration. I could put my practical business experience to good use in the classroom and use my knowledge of business practices as a base for research.

That proved to be only half right. A background in business helped in the classroom, where students eagerly sought to connect abstract principles with real-life situations. But in the critical area of research – the key to tenure and commitment by your employer to lifetime employment – the value of business exposure proved considerably less substantial.

Over time, I perceived the orientation toward the study of business, as reflected in journal articles, books, conferences, and the views held by young new members of the faculty, shifting away from business *per se* toward the study of the "science of business." Instead of furthering a deeper understanding of business practices, in order to improve them, mind-sets began to close around the few untested propositions that were available. Increasing effort was being expended on testing such propositions, and correspondingly there was less emphasis on developing new ideas, or questioning the validity of what was being tested. Barriers against new knowledge were erected, and kept getting higher.

Management, in short was becoming prematurely dogmatic; a trap that economics set for itself in distancing theories from what even casual observation could dispute. Economists did not consciously freeze their models in time. Many economists, Joseph Schumpeter prominent among them, stressed history's lesson of continuous *change*. Yet the causal connection of history with time and place is incompatible with the economist's static model, which assumes general equilibrium: a difference that has worked to the disadvantage of economic history and eventually relegated it to a minor place within conventional economics. Joan Robinson clarified this inherent bias of economic science thus:

> in a model depicting equilibrium positions there is no causation. It consists of a closed circle of simultaneous equations. The value of each element is entailed by the values of the rest. [In contrast] in an historical model, causal relations have to be specified.[3]

Business still has a chance to escape the economist's dilemma. There is no natural law that dictates the advancement of method over meaning. Borrowing the words of a Nobel laureate in economics, the first duty of business "is to describe what is out there: valid description without a deeper explanation is worth a thousand times more than a clever explanation of nonexistent facts."[4]

If interest continues to diminish in expanding the knowledge base of business, and data-driven tests of existing propositions continue to dominate, American industry ultimately will be the loser. How and what business instructors choose to research influences how they communicate in the classroom, which affects what future business leaders will believe and how they will compete.

Fortunately, opinions have not all hardened. Some management scholars have expressed the need for better conceptualization of ideas and less emphasis on rigorous tests of what is presumed to be known.[5] This minority view sees the perceptions of managers as critical to sound strategic analysis and the "firm" deserving of closer attention as the "primary unit of analysis."[6]

As logical as such insights may seem, they face strong opposition from a growing academic community that perceives advantages in a simplified and abstract view of business over the many complexities and uncertainties of the real thing. Realistically, pressures to move business studies closer to the economist's mode of abstraction are not easily resisted. Perhaps the most prominent factor exerting pressure in that direction is the educational system itself.

Biases in the Academic System

On leaving business for business education, I naively believed that what I knew to be true, from practice and experience, would be valuable and transferable into higher education. This, I found, is not necessarily so. Only that part of knowledge that is tractable to an organization's goals is truly useful. Knowing about businesses contributes only incidentally to writing about businesses.

It took a while to appreciate how universities differ from businesses and how these differences create a unique academic culture. Once understood, however, moves to "reorient" business, and business policy in particular, toward the research tradition of economics and the arts and sciences could have been anticipated.

Major universities demand research from members of their faculty, as echoed in the familiar refrain: "publish or perish." But publishing by itself is not enough. Publications must be in the right journals. These, in turn, follow a strict priority. The most highly rated journals typically accept articles that are narrowly specialized and heavily quantified. They also attract the smallest readership.

A barrier of language excludes the average reader. Few crossovers, for instance, exist between math and nonmath literature.[7] Close attention to technique tends to blot out the larger patterns and emerging trends. Instead of being a handicap, obscurity has become the hallmark of the truly scholarly article. Herbert Stein, former chairman of the President's Council of Economic Advisors, protested that when he came to Washington he "could read and reasonably understand almost everything in the economic journals. Today, [he] can read hardly any of it."[8] Contributions of whatever quality or substance seldom reach beyond a small inner circle of scholars and thus remain inaccessible to those the author presumes to study. On average, "articles published in a learned journal have about five readers each," according to one reckoning.[9]

Exclusivity is reinforced as newly qualified PhD holders, whose theses are immersed in the latest scientific methods, are appointed to the editorial boards of journals and proceed to draw standards ever tighter. Smaller and smaller problems receive greater and greater scrutiny. Attention shifts from the importance of being right to the importance of being methodical. In the "top" journals, the significance of the topic, or its impact on advancing knowledge in the field, is almost beside the point.

An emphasis on technical skills is carried over into the classroom as well. New instructors, indoctrinated with an array of quantitative skills without which a PhD is no longer feasible, generally lack real-world training. Compensating for this lack of practical expertise, junior faculty members tend to favor rigorous exposition. As pedagogy, a systematic and precise theory has distinct advantages. Answers are predetermined. Given the fixed logic of a theoretical model, one knows where it leads. Given well-defined problems to address, answers are not only precise, but convincing. Given a choice, new teachers prefer precision over uncertainty, and what can be taught over what must be learned.

Once defined, models are unswervingly faithful to their programmed logic pattern. The logic itself thereafter becomes the subject to be taught, and learned. In sum, models offer elegant simplifications of the almost limitless subjective and complex relationships in the real world. Viewed in terms of pedagogy and apart from possible mis-specifications of the models, "inventing business" is enormously easier than dealing with it as it is.

The preoccupation of young teachers with normative models is understandable, and perhaps unavoidable under the present system. Most instructors progress from student to teacher with no intervening exposure with which to contrast what they have been told or have read. As experience yields to technique, there are more numerative answers than there are quantitative-type questions.

Mathematical skills can thus become more important than mastery of subject matter.[10] In higher education, such skills smooth the way for advancement. A merely competent mathematician stands a better chance of succeeding in higher education, whether in business or economics, as a researcher or teacher, than a chief executive officer from one of America's leading corporations. As one mathematician-turned-economist phrased it: "One could do math while maintaining the credible pretense of relevance by labeling the variables."[11]

Through a Darwinian process of natural selection, there is the danger that over time determinism will triumph over relativism, rationality will win over judgment, objectivity will substitute for intuition, and quantitative language will dominate the study of business. A "scientific" mentality has become important for published research. It also contributes to pedagogical technique and, ultimately, to a faculty member's prospects for promotion and advancement. But is it business? Business shorn of behavioral aspects is Romeo without Juliet. Hiding the imperfections and uncertainties of competition shields students from some of the more challenging aspects of a business career.

Clearly not *all* business problems lend themselves solely to quantitative analysis. Decision-making is not influenced entirely by numbers. Indeed, future-oriented and irreversible decisions, those most critical to a firm's ultimate success or failure, cannot be solved by pure calculus. This point is so obvious as to beg the question: why would institutions dedicated to truth and objectivity perpetuate myths, merely because they are disguised as science?

For an answer, one must look to the special marketplace in which higher education operates. Neither informed consumers nor effective competition exist in the normal sense. Students, as customers, seldom complain. They lack preparation for informed criticism. They pay the price of an education largely on faith. If they fail as future business managers, it is their fault and not that of the system. They are the ones being evaluated, rather than the other way around. Moreover, there is little opportunity for comparison.

Among comparably rated educational institutions, the academic menu is remarkably uniform. There are, of course, financial demands on higher education. Public institutions depend on governmental funds. But on purely academic matters, institutions of higher education are relatively immune from outside review or competitive pressures.

With few external demands for change, and over a normal course of time, the educational system tends to perpetuate and reflect the self-interests of its members: the faculty and administrators. With new business faculty members trained to emulate their peers, the grip of conformity closes ever more firmly. Within a closed system, the prevailing culture wields tremendous power. What separates good scholarship from bad, and myths from reality, depends on the perceptions and beliefs of those who govern.

How Business Education Evolved

From the beginning, business education was viewed with skepticism by scholars in established disciplines. Members of the traditional liberal arts faculty were suspicious of "practical" education. Robert Hutchins, quoted in the report on higher education for business sponsored by the Carnegie Foundation, expressed concern that career preparation of any kind "deprives the university of its only excuse for existence, which is to provide a haven where the search for truth may go unhampered by utility or pressure for results."[12]

A strain of intellectual aloofness has always run deep within higher education. Professional schools like medicine, engineering, and law, and especially business, were foreign to classical scholars. Members of the liberal arts faculty, accustomed by habit and tradition to an academic life of splendid contemplation, never felt comfortable with the application of knowledge.

Faced with the problem of assimilation, school administrators turned for advice, naturally enough, to those they considered closest to business: economists. Parallels between economics and business provided the pretext. Economics covered the general economy and also encompassed the subject matter of business. Although this commonality of interests was in fact more apparent than real, economists were to exert a strong influence on the way business education was perceived, and on ultimate recommendations to change it.

The Influence of Economics on Business Education

Two of the most important studies influencing the development of modern business education were published in 1959 with the support of the Ford

Foundation and the Carnegie Foundation. Both studies were written by economists, who collaborated closely with each other.

The tenor of the reports was condescending and critical throughout. Business was perceived as low level and overly practical in nature, and was deemed in need of major repairs. Standards of business were thought to be embarrassingly inadequate. Business courses in many cases were portrayed as not much more than vocational training. A blue-collar, trade-school image came through as typical in too many institutions, according to the findings.

There was, in truth, considerable ammunition for criticism. Curricula varied widely, including less than demanding courses in secretarial instruction, elementary book-keeping, and clerical tasks. Schools located in the South and Midwest were particularly singled out for censure.

Firms and entrepreneurs instrumental in promoting business education were not always motivated by the advancement of scholarship. Joseph Wharton, a prominent steelmaker and namesake for the Wharton School of Finance and Commerce at the University of Pennsylvania, the first undergraduate school of business in the USA, also counted among his less noble motives the desire to offer an alternative to liberal "free-trade" teachings of that period.[13]

The use of business people as instructors tended to slant course work strongly in favor of application over theory. The general orientation of business education often tended to reflect the specific needs or interests of the business community. The founding of New York University's School of Commerce, Accounts, and Finance in 1900, for example, could be traced to influence exerted by the New York State Society of Certified Public Accountants, who wanted to provide students with the proper accounting background needed to pass the CPA examinations.[14]

There were, in short, a number of points on which the authors of the Carnegie and Ford reports could find fault with the beginnings of business education in the United States. With no explicit blueprint to follow, business programs had groped forward in an experimental trial-and-error fashion. Financial pressures were a continuing concern for administrators of business programs. By necessity, they were forced to lean on business people to staff courses as well as borrow instructors from a variety of other academic departments, often with reluctant acquiescence by those so chosen.

This primitive state of affairs, however, was not indicative of the more progressive schools at the time the Ford and Carnegie studies were released. Before 1940, most major public universities in the country had established a school of business. By 1959, when the conclusions of the two reports were made public, the harshest criticisms had already been remedied in these leading institutions. Curricula were more stringent. Emphasis had shifted from dependence on part-time to full-time instructors and also toward a stronger research orientation. Pioneering schools like Harvard, Pennsylvania, California at Berkeley, Chicago, Northwestern, Dartmouth, Columbia, New York University, and others had already advanced well beyond the rudimentary level on which the two Foundation-sponsored studies concentrated. Had one or several of these schools served as the model for business education, and the authors of the reports on business education been professors of business rather than professors of economics, the future course of business education may well have taken a different turn.

As it was, what was recommended in the Carnegie Foundation and Ford Foundation reports resembled not so much a distinct new approach geared to a specialization in business as a hybrid of existing courses in economics, the humanities, and the sciences. Whether students specialized in economics or business, the recommended course work involved considerable overlap. A heavy dose of economics, mathematics, and statistics, together with a traditional liberal arts emphasis, exemplified the ideal undergraduate curriculum. At graduate level, an analytically rigorous Master in Business Administration degree was proposed to follow a prescribed four-year foundation in the arts and sciences. Preparation for business, it seemed, needed relatively little background, or course work, in business. This philosophy reflected the background and conviction of the authors, who believed that "economics as one branch of the social sciences has traditionally provided the only theoretical framework for the study of business, and even today the two fields are so closely related they can hardly be discussed separately."[15]

The American Assemby of the Collegiate Schools of Business (AACSB) – the chief accreditation agency for business schools – adopted many of the recommendations in the reports. As a consequence, the current number of liberal arts and science credits as a percentage of the total credits required for an education in business is substantial. Those specializing in business studies in accredited business schools typically take at least half, and often more, of their total credits outside their major field. The reasoning presumably was to provide intellectual stimulation, plus a more rounded educational experience.

The soundness of opening one's mind to teachings and ideas from other fields applies in principle to any discipline. The Carnegie Foundation report, for example, expressed concern that although the exclusiveness of a curriculum devoted to business might help achieve a certain identity for business, it tended to isolate it from the rest of the academic community. Though logical, this philosophy seemed reserved for business alone. Neither the two Foundation studies on higher education for business, the 1987 study on management education and development commissioned by the AACSB, nor any study before or since has mentioned the desirability of students specializing in liberal arts or social sciences to take even a single business course, although many of these students eventually find jobs in the private sector. No serious evaluation of business education, to my knowledge, has made an effort to change the impression that enlightenment flows only in one direction.

The academic majority clearly expected that business education would be absorbed into the prevailing orthodoxy of the arts and science departments. What they did not anticipate was the explosive growth in demand for business courses. Despite predictions of a leveling off in business enrollments, the 1960s, 1970s, and 1980s saw continued expansion in business education, and a corresponding contraction in the liberal arts. As its base of influence widened, business assimilated more and more courses formerly taught by staff in other departments. Instead of following the lead of economics in creating a niche within the arts and sciences, as the Carnegie and Ford reports foresaw, business became a dominant and independent educational force.

Business has won a contest of sorts in terms of student popularity. The intellectual battle, however, has barely begun. Economics and business basically look at problems from a different point of view.

As long as economics remained engrossed in macroeconomics, and business was divided along functional lines, the contrasts in outlook were minimized. However, acceptance of business policy as the required capstone course for business, with the firm as the central player, has brought business directly into conflict with the economist's theory of the firm. Because of business policy's interdisciplinary nature – the combination and integration of knowledge from all fields, contributing to the study of general management, including economics – an unavoidable area of intersecting interests arises. Both sides are inexorably and perhaps unwittingly being drawn closer together, accentuating the contrast between economists, who model business behavior, and business strategists, who still try to understand it. Resolution of the inherent conflicts in philosophy and methods cannot be avoided for ever. A minority of economists dissatisfied with the current state of economic microtheory have launched initiatives for new concepts of the firm (about which more will be said later), while management as a discipline has shifted closer to the abstract, quantitative approach of economics.

Nowhere is the contrast between the perspectives of economics and business drawn as sharply as in the way the two disciplines view business firms. In traditional economics, the supposed theory of the firm is not about firms at all. Neither actual firms nor decisions that influence firm behavior have an active part to play.

Coase, an economist who wrote a ground-breaking article on the nature of the firm, placed the emphasis of economics on the price mechanism, with only indirect acknowledgement to the firm:

> The economic system "works itself." This does not mean that there is no planning by individuals. These exercise foresight and choose between alternatives. This is necessarily so if there is to be order in the system. But this theory assumes that the *direction of resources is dependent directly on the price mechanism.*[16]

Business policy, on the other hand, takes a holistic view, with the firm as the centerpiece of analysis. In a classic definition of strategy, Andrews described it as:

> the pattern of objectives, purposes, or goals and major policies and plans for achieving those goals, stated in such a way as to define what business the company is in or is to be and the *kind of company it is or is to be.*[17]

Ostensibly studying the same phenomenon, neither side sees it through the other's eyes. Economists claim a higher intellectual ground based on the rigor of their models, consistent with their determination to be thought of as scientific. This dedication to science exacts a price. Profoundly subjective elements are absent from the models, including consideration of personal psychology, motivations, or expectations. Nor are large corporations, governments, unions, employees, suppliers, or other flesh-and-blood actors explicitly recognized. The theory of the firm is just that, a theory. Or, more bluntly, it is a myth. Nevertheless, it is a very long-lived myth.

For some time, economists have not been overly concerned with their "empty" theory of the firm, because they were concentrating on the greater economic picture. Even now, the economy as a whole preoccupies the economic mainstream and accounts for the majority of material in most conventional textbooks on economics. Yet inattention hardly justifies its longevity. The defense that prevents this particular theory from collapsing under a sheer inadequacy of factual support, and which protects the economics professions generally, is the shield of "science" itself. Pre-empting their critics by claiming a superior methodology, while inferring that anything less is inferior, economists have crafted a powerful argument for disarming their critics. This stratagem of the economists deserves special attention, not for its use in economics, which is not the focus of this book, but for the inclination in business to imitate the arguments and means by which economics has established its reputation for scientific rigor.

The Influence of Science on Economics

There are three phases in conducting scientific research: the formulation of hypotheses, testing, and interpretation. Hypotheses propose what might be true, based on reasonable assumptions that are factually grounded or are not contradicted by known facts. Since a search for truth is the essence of science, any attempt to suppress evidence would contravene and undermine the very basis of scientific inquiry.

In apparent defiance of this common view lies the theory of the firm. Even its strongest advocates do not defend it as based on the actual workings of business or industry in general. What facts are known contradict every assumption underlying the theory: identical products, profusion of very small firms, and freedom of entry and exit. While agriculture is habitually used as a case that approximates this picture of perfect competition, the vast majority of American industry does not even come close to this theory. Products differ widely among firms. Relatively speaking, a few firms account for the bulk of the output in most industrial sectors. Sunk costs and barriers to entry create frictions that impede easy access and exit from industries. On all three counts, perfect competition does not vaguely resemble the actual conditions under which firms operate. Yet this hypothetical depiction of the firm is kept alive by economists. In apparent disregard for the factual basis of science, the textbooks give perfect competition a central role in economic microtheory, indoctrinating students with a model of business that has little or no application outside the classroom.

As a rebuttal, economists generally protest that the theory of the firm does not presume to mirror business in all its particulars. Any general theory must reduce and abstract from a multitude of details. There will inevitably be missing pieces. Moreover, the trade-off between simplification and exactitude is worthwhile, if it enables a greater insight than would otherwise be possible by concentrating too intently on isolated parts of a theoretical puzzle.

So far, this line of reasoning seems arguably fair. Every nuance of a very complicated landscape cannot possibly be surveyed. At the macro-level, especially, this makes some sense. There are so many players and institutions that operations of the overall economy cannot be grasped meaningfully by looking at an infinite number of individual units. At the level of the firm, however, this same argument seems weak. Although all aspects may not be manageable even here, can the principal factor – the firm itself – be omitted from the theory without crippling its credibility?

To outsiders, the lack of empirical support for theoretical propositions in economics questions the central notion of scientific objectivity, around which economics has built its reputation.[18] Economists as a rule do not study institutions. Articles by economists hardly ever mention actual firms or deal with their problems.[19] Economists do not conduct interviews or mail questionnaires. They do not collect primary data to try and under-

monopolistic competition. Although this was developed in the 1930s, as an attempt to inject more realism into economics, Friedman sees monopolistic competion as falling short of the needs of economic science. As a compromise between pure monopoly and perfect competition, it possesses "none of the attributes that would make it a truly useful general theory."[30]

In trying to be more realistic, monopolistic competition introduced imprecision and fuzziness that frustrated the need of economic science for unambiguous statements and results, according to Friedman. For example, if product differentiation is introduced, as in monopolistic competition, the variety of possible classes of products, and the inability to define each class discretely, would make the theory "analytically meaningless."[31] *The very act of moving toward greater realism would defeat the objective of structural precision required in economic science.* Measured against the economist's strict standards, perfect competition and pure monopoly are the only truly suitable models. Monopolistic competition, on the other hand, "offers no tools for the analysis of an industry and so no stopping place between the firm at one extreme and general equilibrium at the other."[32]

Further, Friedman argues that the theory of the firm is misinterpreted. It is not a general theory applicable to the entire business scene. Instead it is a general theory only in the limited area in which it applies. That is, even though extremely limited in scope, its principles remain valid in the narrow circumstances where its implications apply. In effect, the model of the firm is worth preserving because of its perfection, even if such perfection is seldom encountered.

This notion sacrifices relevance for rigor. If a model only works as merely illustrative of what might be, but is far removed from what is, is it important enough to care about, or devote a student's education to, or serve as a guide to policy or personal actions in any significant way? By clinging to a contrived and narrow view, economists are prone to treat the ideas in their models as crucial and facts as mere incidentals.

Had positive economics prevailed in the time of Christopher Columbus, he may never have discovered America. To the naked eye, the earth appears flat. With only crude instruments in Columbus's time, and viewing relatively small parcels of ground, a flat-earth doctrine could be convincingly argued. If no one could disprove this contention, positive economic thinking would argue it to be so. The fact that ships would "disappear" over the horizon might suggest the contrary – but this would not provide sufficient contrary evidence. Neither trips to distant lands, nor circumnavigating the globe would in principle impeach the general notion of flatness. Such observed inconsistencies could not displace a well-constructed general theory. Only a superior alternative theory could do that. Since at the time the techniques for determining the earth's exact contours were not known, the earth's flatness could not be scientifically rejected.

Alas, in the end there is no disproof, only disinterest. Defined small enough, a plot of ground may indeed be flat for all practical purposes and thus arguable *as a hypothesis*. But such a hypothesis serves only as a first conjecture. To ignore evidence of curvature, even though it cannot yet be "scientifically" demonstrated, substitutes ideology for science. Without continuous updating and replacement of old theorems, no real progress would be possible. Economics' Maginot line around perfect theoretical laws may keep them alive, but outside the profession of economics only a few curiosity seekers may find them worth the bother.

Friedman clearly exaggerates when he describes economics as an objective science "in precisely the same sense as any of the physical sciences."[33] Only economics' notion of "science" is based on artificial intelligence rather than hard evidence. Like the physical sciences, economists have concrete "matter" to observe: in firms, industries, managers, etc. Unlike the physical sciences, however, there are no natural laws to uncover. Once postulated, the presumed laws of economics either change with the times or lose their descriptive and predictive accuracy.

Finally, deprecating the value of assumptions opens the way for pseudoscience. At any given time, numerous associations between variables may exist: these associations have validity in a statistical sense, but the findings are spurious and contrary to common sense. The classical economist W. Stanley Jevons developed a correlation between eruptions on the sun's surface and business cycles; the statistical correlation was so strong that he was convinced that it could not be accidental. Even today, prognosticators periodically proclaim discoveries that correlate random variables with changes in business conditions, and the stock market is a favorite object of such analyses. Modern-day pseudoscientists have developed supposedly valid statistical associations linking moves in the stock market with such esoterica as the length of women's hemlines, the width of men's ties and the team that wins the annual Superbowl in football, to name but a few. Economist and Nobel prize-winner Robert Solow claimed: "[I can] verify the existence of witches if you give me the chance every other year to tack on some variables in a regression."[34]

In a complex world, the most important part of science may be the assumptions one starts out with, contrary to Friedman's position. Because economic theories are constructed so as to achieve equilibrium, the answers they give are constrained by what the model specifies. The theory of the firm, for instance, has no power to predict anything contrary to what it postulates. For example, if competition among many small firms has been *postulated* as a condition of the model, then the model cannot be a source for predicting anything more insightful about competition. For economics to be truly useful as a predictive science, it would "have to build 'lawful' postulates and not upon convenient but counterfactual assumptions."[35]

Once economics entertains unrealistic assumptions, it shuts out the real world of business as a field of study. Unwittingly, perhaps, it also opens the way for competing "unrealistic" models to displace orthodox economic theory (see the subsection on rational expectations).

Rational expectations (ratex)   This represents a new wave of economic thought, which threatens to displace mainstream economics. In simple terms, ratex supposes that persons absorb and discount all available information, and react rationally. Whatever government policy might be proposed, for example, will have been neutralized by people's anticipation of its impact, thereby minimizing the role that government can play in economic stabilization. The economy will be regulated automatically and optimally by people acting in their own self-interests; prices will adjust and markets will clear instantaneously to maintain equilibrium as people react negatively or positively to new information. Ratex will guarantee the desired adjustments to keep the economy on an even keel.

Ratex theorists have co-opted Milton Friedman's idea on positive economics, whether consciously or not, in building a competing theory. Starting with a new set of parameters, ratex academicians constructed an internally consistent model of how the economy might work. Since the realism of the assumptions on which ratex is based – complete information rationally and instantaneously acted upon – is not relevant, according to Friedman, the parameters themselves are not challengeable. Also, since a general theory can only be displaced by a superior general theory, proponents in effect are reduced to debating the merits of "my theory versus your theory." In this type of gamesmanship, the edge belongs to the side with the most sophisticated technical solution. Using economics' main weapons of mathematics and statistics, ratex appears to have the upper hand, as quantitative skills outdistance those required by either Keynesians or monetarists, the two main competing bodies of economic orthodoxy.

Whether ratex's model produces useful predictions or not is not of immediate concern. Keynesians and monetarists have survived for many years in spite of repeated forecasting errors and omissions.[36] The blemished records of Keynesianism and monetarism, in fact, lent encouragement to a minority of economists to look elsewhere for answers. Guided by economics' orientation to science, and liberated from fact-based assumptions, ratex provided an alternative outlet for former loyalists.

The economic old guard thus finds itself in a dilemma it helped create. It cannot attack ratex's assumptions as unrealistic without opening its own theories to the same criticism. Nevertheless, faced with the threat of a powerful competitor, Keynesians and monetarists have banded together to denounce ratex's sleek new mathematical models as mentally engaging, but vacuous, relying for refutation on much the same type of arguments that pragmatists used against them. In the end, economists are realists, even if their models are not. Many in the mainstream are now saying in effect that "assumptions *do* matter." In explaining his objections to ratex, Robert Solow concedes that allowing your opponent's assumptions is a trap – one that had been set by Friedman and used in a positive way to ward off criticism from non-economists, but which is now being used by an economic minority against the majority. In an anecdotal manner, Solow points out the dangers in accepting irrational assumptions at face value:

> Suppose someone sits down where you are sitting right now and announces to me that he is Napoleon Bonaparte. The last thing I want to do with him is to get involved in a technical discussion of cavalry tactics at the battle of Austerlitz. If I do that, I'm getting tacitly drawn into the game that he *is* Napoleon. . . . Since I find [the] fundamental framework [of ratex] ludicrous, I respond by treating it as ludicrous – that is, by laughing at it – so as not to fall into the trap of taking it seriously and passing on to matters of technique.[37]

Solow makes a good point: one that applies equally to economics in all guises and at all times.

A clever, but little appreciated tactical effect of Friedman's positive economics has been to shift the burden onto critics to disprove what economists propose, and thereby put antagonists on the defensive. Economists are prolific writers. That is their job. Their sheer force of intellect and articulation are intimidating. Practitioners neither by training nor inclination are prepared to evaluate their work critically. Thus, much of what economists say never gets tested except by other economists subscribing to the same code of scientific procedures. This builds internal strength within the discipline, but distances economics from the world outside. In the long run, economics' circle of influence must either widen, or diminish to a hard core of iconoclasts.

Viewing the Classical Traditions of Economics

In surveying modern economics, one tends to forget its pragmatic beginnings. From Adam Smith's *Wealth of Nations*,[38] published in 1776, to Alfred Marshall's *Principles of Economics*[39] in 1890, political economy was the profession's field of study and economists were more than just academic scholars: Adam Smith was a teacher of moral philosophy, David Ricardo was a stockbroker, and T. R. Malthus was a clergyman. They experienced what they wrote about and they wrote widely on issues concerned with the betterment of contemporary life. Ideas competed in the marketplace of public opinion and the better economists, or at least those remembered in history's reckoning, attempted to sway public opinion by dealing with the policy implications of economics.

Not until the later decades of the nineteenth century did economics take a dramatic turn away from this classical tradition. From 1870 onward, the vast majority of important economists were university professors of economics. They wrote primarily for other scholars in emerging academic journals like the *Journal of Political Economy*, the *Quarterly Journal of Economics*, and the *Economics Journal*. In 1885, the professional association for American economists, the American Economic Association, was founded. Emphasis by then was shifting from teaching to research. From an interdisciplinary perspective, economics was swinging inward, refining the techniques of research and relying more on peer approval as a test of the merit of theory.

The beginning of the end of the era of political economy can be traced to Leon Walras and his *Elements of Pure Economics*, formulated in 1874.[40] Walras expressed the age-old relationship between supply and demand mathematically. He postulated the conditions for general equilibrium, assuming that actions of markets reflected the utility-maximizing behavior of individuals. By means of simultaneous equations, Walras showed how product prices automatically and instantaneously adjusted to factor prices. His theory was completely static. Given fixed relationships among quantifiable variables, a deterministic solution was assured. Schumpeter proclaimed Walra's *Elements* as "nothing less than the Magna Carta of exact economics."[41]

Since the late nineteenth century, the mathematics of marginal utility theory has been the dominant theme in economics. Although Walras saw his method only as a tool for viewing economic behavior, the beauty of mathematics proved irresistible to fellow economists. Once reduced to quantities, what could previously be approximated in less powerful language could now be expressed with absolute certainty.

Not satisfied to break with the past, modern economics tries to forget it ever had one. Economic history, institutionalism, and political economy have all been expunged from mainstream respectability. Economic history, once deemed essential to an understanding of economics, not only is not seen as useful, but it is taken as a sign of failure to achieve the level of proficiency necessary for really meaningful work and "best left to those underendowed for fully professional work at the modern level."[42]

None of the art of economics has survived. The authoritative definition of economics as the study of human behavior[43] bears no resemblance to the robot-like responses in current economic theory that fail "to reach down to the deep roots of human conduct."[44] Real persons have fared no better in economics than real firms.

The Import of Economics' Past for the Future of Business Education

Management faces its own crossroads. It can follow the example of economics and choose to develop its left brain only: the science of management. However, this would not implement the mission of business schools: to train persons for the practice of management and develop new knowledge that can be applied to the operation of a business.[45] Moreover, it would offer no new contribution, merely imitating in one form or another what economics is already doing.

On the other hand, management has the opportunity to build a credible alternative tradition. In contrast to the positivism of economics, management should accept the uncertainty and seeming irrationality inherent in business decision-making. Theories should not try to be airtight, but rather conditional on a reasonable set of assumptions, which themselves could change over time and would not necessarily exclude competing theories based on different assumptions. Rigorous deductive reasoning, supported by references to real institutions and actions of real people, would address practical problems of management. Theories would be the basis for empirical testing, rather than created out of the test results themselves. Assumptions, once again, would be central to theory-building, with broad support, both from peer acceptance and among the involved public or private constituencies, together with empirical evidence, as the litmus test for the survivability of a proposed theory. Accepting Milton Friedman's contention that economic activity is too diverse to bend wholly to factual description, the question is whether it is best to analyze imperfectly what occurs, and keep refining it, or to hold out for a perfect, but static model, which need not meet any external test of its validity.

In economics, the internal mechanics of the theory of the firm have remained immutable and thus still force the conclusion that Adam Smith's theory of perfect competition, descriptive of an economy of small merchants, still describes the megacorporations of today. Such a representation defies belief. Yet if one steps outside the model, there is no map to follow. When new problems arise, or old certainties die, questions arise for which no answers have been anticipated. An economist's first duty is to the consistency of models. Economists are bound by methodology, rather than events. Observed imperfections, no matter how glaring, seldom shake economists free of their hypotheses. A renowned monetarist, when asked what it would take to change his monetarist views, replied that he would have to change his views if monetary expansion over two or three years did not produce an increase in the rate of inflation.[46] Subsequently, during a period lasting more than three years, the money supply grew, while prices remained relatively stable. As a consequence, prominent economists outside academia, including Beryl Sprinkel, President Reagan's chairman of the Council of Economic Advisors, and an avowed monetarist, recanted doctrinaire positions on monetary policy. Yet among academic economists, a single-minded belief in the power of money is held as fervently as before. Nor has the economist of whom the question was asked stopped being a staunch monetarist.

Sociologists have a name for this imperviousness to criticism – they call it cognitive dissonance. Economists have built a teflon shield around a set of shared beliefs, or myths, that allows the profession to ignore external criticism. As long as economists stay within the constraints of their hypothetical models, the realities of the world outside have no bearing. The danger, of course, is in increasing the remoteness over time between theory and truth.

Business managers, however, cannot avoid real problem-solving. They must deal with all contingencies. Some problems are routine, but the most important ones are not. To survive, firms must cope with the unexpected. They need to understand causal forces for change. How and why individual units interact is more important than constructing relationships that force a predictable answer.

A Three-Pronged Approach Towards the Study of Firm Competition

A first step management must take in creating its own framework of firm competition and behavior is to lower mathematics from its pedestal. Another requirement is to develop a set of standards for judging the quality of new management concepts. Abandoning one approach as inappropriate should not be read as an open invitation to advance nostrums and hearsay as knowledge. The three guidelines below – history, empiricism, and common sense – are proposed as a set of standards for testing the quality of new ideas. They are intended to weed out merely idle speculations, while allowing latitude for new and creative exceptions to the conventional wisdom.

History

Business history is conspicuous by its absence as a required course in the curricula of many schools of business. This slight is more than incidental, since the insights on current management practices build on past trends. Since business history is a neglected field of management, the research forthcoming to fill this gap is modest, and inadequate to the task. Without a sound historical record, intuition, judgement, or imagination may substitute for facts. This is an unenviable position to defend from the viewpoint of scholarship and a presumed ability to convey a "common body of knowledge" that qualifies graduates of business schools as experts in management.

Alfred Chandler, the eminent business historian from Harvard University, almost singlehandedly developed the reference points in business history on which management researchers must rely. His two famous books, *Strategy and Structure* and *The Visible Hand*, explore in depth the way in which modern business enterprise arose and grew.[47] Chandler's work remains singular in chronicling the rise of modern business and the brand of managerial capitalism that characterized it. Although other historians had amassed considerable works on business institutions and individual entrepreneurs, Chandler marveled that "none have written about the rise of modern business enterprise and the brand of managerial capitalism that accompanied it."[48]

Chandler was noticeably kind to management theorists in not dwelling on their oversight of business history. Only at the conclusion of his major work on business strategy and structure did he remark on an inexplicable tendency to treat firms operating in a market economy almost without comment on the changing nature of the market. It seemed strange to him that concepts of business such as leadership, communications, and planning could be studied with only passing reference to their changing environment.[49]

Small wonder that Chandler's research was so enthusiastically received. The void he entered was vast, and it is still gaping. Chandler's observations on the lack of attention given to institutional changes and transformations of business firms still ring true.

As soon as a theory is formalized, for example, it begins to age. Unless continually monitored and updated, its veracity diminishes. What may have been true, or approximately true, invariably loses descriptive accuracy over time. Institutions change, as do people. Adam Smith, for instance, when writing his *Wealth of Nations*, could not conceivably have foreseen the changes in the next 200 years, and if he could, it would have been inconceivable that he would have written the *Wealth of Nations* as he did. As Berle and Means aptly put it: "more could be learned . . . by studying the motives of Alexander the Great, seeking new worlds to conquer, than by considering the petty tradesman of the days of Adam Smith."[50]

The predictive ability of any theory relies on its connection and consistency with what went before. Despite this assistance of history in preparing for the future, there has been little progress in merging business history into business education.

Even with Chandler's own considerable input, the light coverage afforded business enterprise by historians, economists, and management scholars leaves a number of specific research areas uncovered. Chandler's exceptional studies, for example, need to be supplemented and confirmed. A historian, no matter how meticulous or objective, cannot avoid picking and choosing among the facts in developing a particular scenario of events. Single instances of scholarship cannot hope to keep pace with an ever-changing industrial scene. Only by elevating the status accorded to business history can well-researched future studies emphasizing the emergence of modern business enterprise be expected.

In this regard, the AACSB is not helpful. Nowhere in the accreditation standards established by the AACSB are students of business made to take a single course in business history. More likely, the typical business student will sign up for United States or European history, or perhaps economic history, to satisfy the credits demanded in this field. Each branch of history has value in its own right, but none satisfies the need for a separate course in business history. What exposure a student currently receives in business history is generally confined within the context of other business courses and limited to brief comments on the accomplishments of specific individuals in the history of management thought, such as Frederick Taylor, Frank Gilbreth, Elton Mayo, etc.

The Carnegie Foundation's sponsored study of higher education for business made no mention of, or recommendation for, business history at either an undergraduate or postgraduate level. The Ford Foundation, in the similar report published under its auspices, recommended twelve hours of either economic or business history, but only in the first two years prior to admission into a business program. Thus, the study of business history remains conspicuous by the very slight emphasis it is given.

What is needed is a continuous reminder of the changing business scene, as seen from a historical perspective: the "contemporarization of history," if you like. The bulk of this work should come from schools of business, rather than having to draw from other areas in order to enrich business's own proclaimed field of expertise. And the only practical path to realizing this objective is if business history is granted recognition as a basic requirement for a well-rounded education in business education.

Empiricism

The test of business theory ultimately depends on confirmation of supporting evidence. The more documentation that can be mustered and the broader the consensus, the more likely it is that a principle of management is well founded. Management, as well as economics, builds on certain core principles. Once agreed, additional research spreads out from these anchors of knowledge to broaden and deepen the field.

There is basic agreement on avoiding generalizations in research that are not well grounded in logic or fact. This, in turn, leads to rejection of unsupported hypotheses. Even if a proposition is the best that scientific methods can devise, it still is not presumed good enough, if it is not supported by evidence.[51] Although this fundamental rule is noncontroversial, the means of compliance vary widely.

In management, theories based on fixed relationships among a few variables do not form a sufficient methodology to develop the field. The scenery continually changes. New players, new rules, and different motivations pertain in different places and at different times. Unlike the physical sciences, there are no absolutes. Therefore, confirming findings by exact replication procedures in the same way as a physics or chemistry laboratory experiment is not possible.

For example, initial hypotheses in a physical science experiment subsequently may prove to be in error. However, once a number of experiments replicate and reconfirm an initial finding, its constancy is established for all time. Aristotle once taught that the velocity of falling objects was proportionate to their weights. Simon Stevin and later Galileo proved this wrong. Subsequently, no serious student sided with Aristotle's views. It is now uncontested that the acceleration of a body dropped in a vacuum is a constant. As with any natural "law," scientists can build on this base without continually retesting the theorem.

This stability gives science its power. A known quantity will be the same tomorrow as it was yesterday. In business or economics, however, phenomena are always in transition. Today's economy is far different from what it was for Adam Smith, or Alfred Marshall, or John Maynard Keynes. The most fundamental of economic principles – the "law" of supply and demand – has evolved far beyond its classical origins because the underlying forces that affect both supply and demand have dramatically changed. But the notation can still be written as: $S=f(D)$. Expressed mathematically, the relationship seems precise and immutable. This very essence of mathematics is what disqualifies it for attacking certain dynamic issues of management.

In surveying the composition of an industry, for instance, a sample of firms used in one year may not be exactly reconstituted in subsequent years, because of mergers, divestitures, liquidations, or other major restructuring moves. Such recomposition not only alters the nature of the industry being observed, but also the way the new members of the industry choose to operate. Further, it frustrates the ability of researchers to replicate prior studies exactly and thereby unqualifiedly "prove" – in the same manner as the physical sciences – what is postulated as good theory.

A high level of changeability in the structures of industry and uncertainty in firm behavior require researchers to choose their investigative techniques accordingly. Lacking the constancy of natural order, there must be flexibility in order to describe and capture a moving panorama of experiences. Yet a framework that is too loose, that can be stretched to accommodate an infinite number of interpretations, would be of dubious value.

The implication for general management is to seek diversity: diversity in research methods as well as multiplicity of principles, rather than a single overarching scheme. No central view of business can do justice to the multidimensions of policy. Nor is it necessary to express mathematically what can and should be directly observed and recorded. The stress on rigid scientific procedures – which *assume away* the reality of business experience and quantify, measure, and verify a simulated version – seems clearly to have been overdone. Persisting in this direction raises a barrier to the generation of new knowledge and new creative insights, with little net contribution in exchange.

What, then, should represent the art of management? One possibility is to stress more historical research. The contributions of Alfred Chandler not only illuminate the past, but provide historical precedence as a test of the consistency and logic of current practices. Without added research in this vein, management will be ahistorical, anchored only in the present and having a point-in-time validity.

Case studies can also make a contribution to business research. The report on higher education in business sponsored by the Ford Foundation affirmed the value of the case method. "Live" cases based on current problems drawn from the experience of business managers in their own firms were seen as desirable tools for analyzing business policy.[52] Developed in sufficient numbers and in rich detail, a growing body of cases would eventually point to certain strategic responses associated with organizations sharing similar problems. For instance, a single case on an organizational strategy developed in response to a specific environmental pressure – proposed water-pollution standards, let us say – would give limited guidance for policy, except in the unlikely event that this particular situation was again confronted. However, given a sufficient number of cases in which such environmental pressures were a factor, a normative, empirically supportable framework of strategic response could be articulated for that contingency. Eventually, the case files would be extensive enough to describe how managers generally would react under given conditions. A number of examples of rigorous research cases – as opposed to mere descriptive incidents – are available, although they lack the follow-on analyses and comparative research to extrapolate the findings.[53]

Questionnaire surveys, personal interviews, and secondary-source data all have a place in research, if they are conducted carefully and tailored to throw light on well-defined questions of business policy. Biographies and autobiographies of entrepreneurs and bureaucratic managers are likewise valuable. Although these are seldom scholarly in tone, experiences of front-line managers can provide material unavailable to the academic researcher. Unfortunately, there is a tendency to label as inferior anything that is not developed within the community of academic scholars. Seldom will one find reference to managerial writings or experiences in academic work. Even Peter Drucker, perhaps the most widely read and respected authority on management as rated by the business professionals themselves, pays the price for his popularity by being excluded in the citations of highly respected academic journals.[54]

In sum, research methods may be good or bad, depending on how thoughtfully the methodology is carried out. But a more important question is whether the research says anything useful. Did it have. policy implications, either current or future, that would advance the ability of business firms to perform? There are, it seems, two questions one can ask, in addition to verifying the proper procedures, before passing on the value of research: (1) Is there a persuasive factual basis for the conclusions? (2) Do the facts draw on, or refer to, observable phenomena?[55]

In evaluating the relative contributions of quantitative versus qualitative research, the comments of Dr Richard Cyert, President of Carnegie-Mellon University, are worth quoting: "one reason we had better managers than anybody else for a long time was not because we had *better* business schools, it was because we had business schools. People could attend classes, read articles and books, think about management problems, and educate themselves."[56]

Common Sense

Last, but not least, is the test of common sense. Are theories believable? Are they sensible, once stripped of arcane language and symbolism?

In a complicated world with few simple answers, theory begins with a selective vision of what is probable, subject to refinement and testing of this initial perception. Algorithms cannot eliminate the underlying uncertainties. At bottom, there is little worth saying in business or economics that cannot be stated in plain English. Oppenheimer once said that "science is the adaptation of commonsense."[57] In even plainer language, Samuelson claimed that "economic regularities that have no commonsense core that you can explain to your wife will soon fail."[58] Schumpeter saw originality in economics as based on ideology "almost by definition."[59] Friedman perceived that the background of researchers "is not irrelevant to the judgements they reach."[60]

The plain fact is that much of what passes for accepted doctrine lacks empirical foundation. Once formulated, however, and put into a mathematical format, ideology may survive repeated factual assaults. Fallacies proposed as theories may continue "without a cupful of evidence," if ciphered so that they escape outside scrutiny and judgement.[61]

Nonmathematical postulates, on the other hand, must meet the test of experience and common sense: do they accord with what is known? The widely accepted notion of "bounded rationality" developed by Herbert Simon, for example, asks for an intuitive acceptance of Simon's general proposition that individuals have limits on their information-processing capabilities. In support of Simon's view of managerial behavior, Chester Barnard, himself a famous author on business as well as a former president of a large business organization, believed Simon's suppositions, not because of formal proofs, but because they expressed "aspects of [his] experience under a wide variety of conditions."[62]

Strict abstractionism seldom resolves anything truly important. Where more than one position is possible – as in capitalism versus socialism, monetarism versus Keynesianism, and diversification versus specialization – one's preference clearly is influenced by ideology or experience. This is altogether proper. Conviction precedes formal analysis. Rigorous tests of unlikely hypotheses make little sense. Business students, forced to learn through textbooks, rather than on the job, at first substitute learning for knowledge. Only after gaining work experience can they begin to separate what was taught from what can be practically applied.

Nowhere is practical know-how as indispensable as at the chief-executive level of an organization. At this uppermost level in organizations, actions are guided by "persistent habitual experience that is often called intuitive."[63]

Herbert Simon's example of a chess experiment demonstrates the role of intuition in making decisions. Grand masters and novices in chess were asked to view actual chess patterns briefly. Upon removal of the chess board, grand masters reproduced from memory on average 23 or 24 (of about 25) pieces onto their proper squares. The novices replaced only about 6 pieces. Yet when the pieces were arranged randomly on the chess board, the grand masters only duplicated the same number of pieces (about 6) as the novices.

What explains the difference? For the expert exposed to hundreds or thousands of games, the actual game layouts represented familiar patterns. But when the chess pieces were displayed randomly, no familiar frame of reference existed. It is pattern recognition based on repetition that serves experienced business managers as well as grand masters in chess. And it is such patterns of behavior that organizational management must discern in order to understand business operations first, before leaping to make recommendations for improvement.

From earlier times, the emphasis in problem-solving has shifted from disciplined logic and common sense, supported by a few scientific tools, to where the tools dominate the analytical process. Today, to be a successful academic, one must often suppress common sense. How much better it would be, for advances in theory as well as actual practice, if common sense and technique complemented one another, rather than one driving out the other.

History, Empiricism, and Common Sense as Measures of Competitive Behavior

Nowhere is there more need for better understanding than with regard to the competitive behavior among firms. The puzzle of how firms compete, and what factors decide the future structure of inter-firm rivalry, is missing many pieces critical to its solution. Although the theory of perfect competition persists in economics textbooks and in the classrooms, it has failed the test of the market. Competition among a multitude of powerless, small firms has clearly become an outdated notion. In no area has economics been so out of touch as in keeping pace with the growth and development of firms.[64]

For a time, antitrust laws seemed to be favoring economics' view of competition. Passage of the Sherman antitrust statutes served to check growth through mergers – a favorite tactic for quick expansion and greater market power. This gave credence to the economist's belief that the way to maintain competitive efficiency was to restrict the size of firms. But legal barriers proved only a temporary defense to an ongoing, historical bent of firms to grow in size and consolidate their market power. By the middle of the 1950s, companies were experimenting with unrelated diversification, acquiring businesses operating in completely different industries. This type of inter-industry merger activity mushroomed, partly as a consequence of an absence of legal defenses to stop it. Convinced that no economic benefits arose from such unrelatedness, economics had not provided antitrust lawyers with a theoretical basis for stopping the movement. Economists watched helplessly as firms sought to grow by the one main channel outside economists' "conceptual framework."[65]

More recently, the pressures for growth have exploded the traditional constraints on intra-industry mergers as well. Mergers among large competitors in oil, food, soft drink, computers, electronics, and other industries went unchallenged. As early as 1974, the "academic consensus on antitrust had collapsed."[66] By the 1980s, almost all of the old policy guidelines were breached. The Justice Department's antitrust division was operating without an economic rudder and economists, unable theoretically to get to grips with the new realities, had little in the way of policy advice to offer.

Management scholars have also been negligent. They have provided no satisfactory explanation of the continuing strategy of diversification and restructuring. Rather, they have been mainly content to grind out statistical studies comparing the financial performance of diversified firms with undiversified firms, hoping to discover by indirection whether diversification makes sense. That the findings have been inconclusive should come as no surprise. An evolving phenomenon, such as a reordering of industrial structures, can only be statistically rationalized after it stops. While it is taking place, some financial results will look good, some will look bad, and a lot of inconclusive mid-range cases will further confuse the readings. If any conclusive "proof" arises in such circumstances, the investigator's methods or motives probably need re-examination.

What has been sidestepped so far is a serious effort to build a framework of firm growth connected to firms' practices, involving data collection and interpretation as first steps. Also, large global and multidivisional enterprises deserve more emphasis than they are getting because they are increasingly dictating the terms of national and international competitiveness.

Visualizing the firm of the future means relaxing the criteria of a strict scientific research methodology. The meticulous measurement of data must give way to creative thought. Data alone are not enough. New frameworks require new learning and new ways of thinking. Just as Alfred Chandler demonstrated the link between strategy and ensuing structural adaptations, so business must now interpret the strategies that firms have already put into motion. Because diversification broadly defined is so instrumental in firm growth, it is used in this book as a proxy for a "theory of the firm," a more encompassing, but slippery description for firm behavior.

The Structure for the Rest of the Book

Chapters 3 and 4 deal with diversification as a primary motive behind firm behavior and growth. The discussion is divided into two parts: what firms are inclined to do (chapter 3) and what they should be doing (chapter 4). This split is made in order to separate how things actually work from a constructed logic of how they can be made better. Although it is neglected in many studies, this separation seems fundamental. Before offering suggestions for change, an understanding of what moves the present system seems a necessary precondition.

Before dealing with diversification head-on, however, chapter 2 takes up some of the myths that repeatedly surface whenever firms' actions obviously and directly contradict theoretical ideals. Current myths serve to explain away the practices of firms as temporary, or unsound, or illusory.

Having held off an accommodation with the facts for so long, these myths are not easily dislodged. Confronting them is necessary, however, before crafting a new framework of diversification.

Notes

1 Robert A. Gordon and James Howell, *Higher Education for Business* (Columbia University Press, New York, 1959), especially p. 206.
2 Frank C. Pierson, *The Education of American Businessmen* (McGraw-Hill, New York, 1959).
3 Joan Robinson, *Essays in the Theory of Economic Growth* (Macmillan, London, 1962), p. 26.
4 Paul A. Samuelson, "A brief post-Keynesian survey," in *Keynes' General Theory: Reports of Three Decades*, ed. Robert Lekachman (St Martin's Press, New York, 1964), p. 339.
5 James W. Frederickson, "Evaluating the last five years of strategic management research," transcript of a symposium at the Academy of Management's Annual meeting in Chicago, 1986. Published as working paper SC#60 (Columbia University School of Business, New York, 1987).
6 John McGee and Howard Thomas, "Strategic group analysis and strategic management," in *Strategic Management Research: A European Perspective*, eds McGee and Thomas (John Wiley, Chichester, 1986), p. 166.
7 Michael Jensen, "Organization theory and methodology," *Accounting Review*, 58 (1983), pp. 319–39 esp. pp. 332–9.
8 Herbert Stein, *Washington Bedtime Stories* (Free Press, New York, 1986), p. 13.
9 Alec Cairncross, *Economics and Economic Policy* (Basil Blackwell, Oxford, 1986), p. 30.
10 Jonathan Hughes, *The Vital Few*, expanded edn (Oxford University Press, Oxford, 1986), p. X.
11 *Wall Street Journal*, 21 April 1987, p. 72. The article concerned Glenn C. Loury, a professor at Harvard, who had majored in mathematics, but received a doctorate in economics from the Massachusetts Institute of Technology.
12 Robert Hutchins, quoted in Pierson, *Education of American Businessmen*.
13 *Wall Street Journal*, 27 March 1981. As reported in David D. Van Fleet and Daniel A. Wren, "The teaching of history in collegiate schools of business," *Collegiate News and Views* (Winter 1982–3), pp. 17–25.
14 Pierson, *The Education of American Businessmen*, p. 36.
15 Ibid., p. 211.
16 Ronald Coase, "The nature of the firm," *Economica*, 4 (1937), pp. 386–405; extract quoted in the text from p. 387, my italics.
17 Kenneth Andrews, *The Concept of Corporate Strategy* (Dow Jones-Irwin, Homewood, Ill., 1971), p. 3, my italics.
18 Herbert Simon, "New developments in the theory of the firm," *American Economic Review: Papers and Proceedings*, 52 (May 1962), p. 8. Simon takes pains to "emphasize strongly that neither the classical theory of the firm nor any of the amendments to it or substitutes for it that have been proposed have any substantial amount of empirical testing."
19 Wassily Leontief, "Academic economics," *Science*, 217 (4555) (9 July 1982), p. 104, 107. Leontief surveyed articles in the *American Economic Review* from

1972 to 1981 and found that only 1 percent were empirical analyses based on data that had been researched by the author. See also Andrew Hacker, *The Corporation Take-over* (Harper & Row, New York, 1964), p. 71–2. "Ever since [Hacker] became aware of the limited basis of classical theory [he has] sought cases where a classical scholar has made a *significant* theoretical point which would apply to a factory economy and could not apply to an atomistic economy. So far, prior to Keynes, [he] found only a single case."

20 Simon, "New developments in the theory of the firm," p. 11.
21 Milton Friedman, *Essays in Positive Economics* (University of Chicago Press, Chicago, 1953).
22 Ibid., p. 23.
23 Paul A. Samuelson and Herbert Simon, "Problems of methodology – discussion," *American Economic Review: Papers and Proceedings*, 53 (May 1963), pp. 231–6 and 229–31.
24 James Tobin, in Arjo Klamer, *Conversations with Economists* (Rowman and Allanheld, New Jersey, 1983), p. 105.
25 Simon, "Problems of methodology," p. 230.
26 Samuelson, "Problems of methodology," p. 233.
27 As to why business people do not write in economic journals, I am reminded of Herbert Stein's recollection of the answer given by a woman when asked why her 20-year-old son was carried from the car to the apartment house by the chauffeur: "Of course he can walk, but thank God he doesn't have to." In *Washington Bedtime Stories*, p. 13.
28 Robert Lekachman, *Economist at Bay* (McGraw-Hill, New York, 1976), p. 256.
29 Hicks has pointed out that attacks on the theory of the firm would wreck the "greater part of general equilibrium theory," which can hardly be contemplated until something is available to take its place. J. R. G. Hicks, *Value and Capital*, 2nd edn (Clarendon Press, Oxford, 1946), p. 84.
30 Friedman, *Essays in Positive Economics*, p. 38.
31 Ibid., p. 38.
32 Ibid., p. 39.
33 Ibid., p. 14.
34 Solow, quoted in Klamer, *Conversations with Economists*, p. 136.
35 Sidney Schoeffler, *The Failures of Economics: A Diagnostic Study* (Harvard University Press, Cambridge, Mass., 1955), pp. 84–5.
36 Andrew M. Kamarck, *Economics and the Real World* (Basil Blackwell, Oxford, 1983), pp. 72–3.
37 Solow, quoted in Klamer, *Conversations with Economists*, p. 146.
38 Adam Smith, *An Inquiry into the Nature and Causes of the Wealth of Nations* (University of Chicago Press, Chicago, 1976).
39 Alfred Marshall, *Principles of Economics*, 8th edn (Macmillan, London, 1961).
40 Leon Walras, *Elements of Pure Economics*, tr. W. Jaffe (George Allen and Unwin, London, 1954).
41 Joseph A. Schumpeter, as mentioned in Daniell Bell and Irving Kristol, *The Crisis in Economic Theory* (Basic Books, New York, 1982), p. 52.
42 George J. Stigler, *The Economist as Preacher* (University of Chicago Press, Chicago, 1982), p. 107.
43 Lionel Robbins, *An Essay on the Nature and Significance of Economic Science*, 2nd edn (London, 1932), p. 16.
44 G. L. S. Shackle, *The Nature of Economic Thought* (Cambridge University Press, London, 1966), p. 31.

45 Gordon and Howell, *Higher Education for Business*, ch. 3, esp. p. 47.
46 Alfred D. Chandler, Jr, *Strategy and Structure* (MIT Press, Cambridge, Mass., 1962).
47 Alfred D. Chandler, Jr, *The Visible Hand* (Belknap Press, Cambridge, Mass., 1977).
48 Ibid., p. 5.
49 Chandler, *Strategy and Structure*, p. 396.
50 Adolf A. Berle and Gardiner C. Means, *The Modern Corporation and Private Property* (Harcourt Brace, New York, 1968), p. 308 (1st edn, 1932).
51 Samuelson, "Problems of Methodology," p. 236.
52 Gordon and Howell, *Higher Education for Business*, p. 207.
53 David J. Hickson, Richard J. Butler, David Cray, Geoffrey R. Mallory, and David C. Wilson, "Comparing 150 decision processes," in *Organizational Strategy and Change*, ed. Johannes M. Pennings and Associates (Jossey-Bass, San Francisco, Calif., 1985), pp. 114–42, esp. pp. 116–17.
54 Frederickson, "Evaluating the last five years of strategic management research," pp. 52–5. Of the fifty most-cited strategy works of 1980–5 not a single work by Peter Drucker was included.
55 These were the two criteria needed to be asked of a set of assumptions in economics, according to Joan Robinson, *Economics is a Serious Subject* (Heffer, Cambridge, 1932), p. 6.
56 Richard M. Cyert, "CEO roundtable," *Outlook*, 10 (1987), p. 40.
57 R. Oppenheimer, "Analogy in science," *American Psychologist*, 11 (1956), p. 129.
58 Samuelson, "Problems of methodology," p. 235.
59 Joseph A. Schumpeter, *History of Economic Analysis* (Oxford University Press, New York, 1954), p. 42.
60 Friedman, *Essays in Positive Economics*, p. 30.
61 Stigler, *The Economist as Preacher*, p. 19. Stigler's comments were made in reference to Frank Knight's (his economics instructor) ethical, but empirically unsupported, judgments against the claims of the competitive economic systems. Two further claims against the competitive system that *were* substantiated, but ignored, are: R. L. Hall and C. J. Hitch, "Price theory and business behaviour," *Oxford Economic Papers*, 2 (1939), pp. 12–45. (In a sample of thirty-eight manufacturing firms, the authors found that prices were not set by equating marginal cost with marginal revenue, as theory implies, but that many firms seemed to set prices based on costs plus mark-up for overhead and profit.) See also Robert Lanzillotti, "Pricing objectives in large companies," *American Economic Review*, 48(5) (1958), pp. 921–40. (The author's study concluded that no single hypothesis such as profit maximization nor a general theory like the theory of the firm provided a satisfactory basis to explain price behavior.)
62 Chester I. Barnard, "Foreword," in Herbert Simon, *Administrative Behavior*, 3rd edn (Free Press, New York, 1976), p. xiv.
63 Chester I. Barnard, *The Functions of the Executive*, 2nd edn (Harvard University Press, Cambridge, Mass., 1968), p. 291.
64 Edith T. Penrose, *The Theory of the Growth of the Firm* (Basil Blackwell, Oxford, 1972), p. 1. To her knowledge, "no economist has as yet attempted a general theory of the growth of firms."
65 Robert Solo, "New maths and old sterilities," *Saturday Review*, 22 January 1972, p. 47.
66 Kenneth Davidson, *Megamergers* (Ballinger, New York, 1985), p. 117.

2
Six Deadly Management Myths

Strategic management (the modern term for business policy) needs to stake out its own theoretical position. Without a specific research tradition, strategic management risks being the stepchild of other disciplines, with theories proposed for it by others. In order to set its own theoretical boundaries, and develop its own assumptions, strategic management must create an initiative to develop its own distinguishing characteristics.

At the very heart of strategic management lies the need to understand how firms and industries behave. Because economics also holds a developed position on firm behavior, its ideas have potential application in general management. That is why economists' views get considerable attention. There is, however, a corollary concern with too close an identification with economics' beliefs. Economics is committed to a methodology that is exact, but inflexible. By emphasizing optimum solutions achieved through the perfect functioning of markets, economists have excused themselves from studying the actions of institutions and individuals within the markets. In a market-oriented approach, managers of organizations merely execute the orders given through the markets. Strategic management, by comparison, assumes that managerial decisions and firm strategies can make a difference. Over time, the choice of strategic options determines which firms adapt and which fall by the wayside. In contrast, epochal changes in the conditions of firms and industries in this century have passed virtually without comment in the textbooks and theories of economics.

The paramount and unreplicatable advantage of strategic management, relative to economics, is its freshness. Its slate is relatively clean. There is opportunity to rethink and recreate a way of looking at problems unfettered by an obligation to the past.

A vital area in need of new understanding is the theory of the firm. This is the aim of this and succeeding chapters. It stops short of developing a full-blown theory, but focuses instead on developing a key part of overall firm strategy: diversification. Technically, an overarching theory of the firm presents an intimidating, if not impossible undertaking. John Maynard Keynes's *General Theory*, published in 1935, was the last attempt at synthesis on such a grand scale. That effort attempted to coalesce opinions from within the single discipline of economics. Trying to satisfy the various disciplines that would lay claim to a piece of a new theory of the firm may be beyond the genius or persuasive powers of any single individual.

While narrowing the scope of study, diversification strategy would still deal with critical issues of firm evolution and competition. It would focus on large, complex organizations that are relatively under-researched. It automatically makes the firm the proper unit of analysis. Further, a study of diversification invariably converges with theories of managerial motivation, firm evolution, strategic groupings, and industry structures. As such, diversification offers a rubric under which complementary, but currently isolated streams of research can be assimilated.

Just as importantly, the formulation of a new strategy of diversification means rebutting certain prevailing assumptions that are commonly held. Without taking this step, one remains subject to contradictory views that cannot be summarily dismissed and that generally are strongly defended.

The several "myths" discussed in this chapter include cherished and often-repeated claims of both economics and management theorists. As counter-evidence, I will rely on management practices. In economics, the omission of real firms, real managers, and real problems seems a singular oversight. For management to take the same course would seriously compound the error. To paraphrase a famous economist, I will use plausible premises to reach reasonable conclusions. Although this approach has shortcomings, it is preferable to the alternative: "the building of irrefutable theorems into an empty edifice of compounded tautologies."[1]

Myth 1: Industries are Stable

Both classical and modern economic theory treat industry structures as stable and change as the exception. This unexamined assertion of economics is also shared to a lesser degree by strategic management. Because the case for economics influences the development of management's own logic, a brief review of economic thought comes first.

One of the tenets of perfect competition, interestingly enough, is freedom of entry and exit of firms. On the surface, this would appear to provide justification for industries to restructure and change over time. But this is not what economists mean. Once formed, industries are not presumed to change. Freedom of entry and exit refers to movement from within by competing firms, or from outside investment in new plant and equipment, in order to keep competitive pressures on profits, but it is not meant to affect industry boundaries and is certainly not contemplative of one firm leaving its core industry in order to cross over into a completely new industry. In classical economics, a notion of firm diversification beyond original products and markets was never envisioned; nor could writers of that period reasonably be expected to have forecast such an occurrence.

Once economics was committed to an emphasis on static equilibrium, dynamic behavior at the firm and industry levels could not be introduced without upsetting the limiting conditions of equilibrium theory. Specifically, static models could not analyze shifts in industry structures through time. Points in time could be handled, but not the interim moves to connect them. Literally, modern economics still cannot explain how to get there from here. In settling for equilibrium, economics lost sight of entrepreneurial capitalism, dynamics of markets, and real competitive forces. As a practical matter, industry shifts were not denied so much as ignored. Market definitions on which a theory of diversification depends received "virtually no attention from economists."[2]

Strategic management's analysis of industry sructures is not so closely bound to tradition, Strategists have the benefit of historic hindsight. With many generations of business experience to build on, strategic management could be expected to avoid the shortcomings of economic theory. In many respects, this has proved to be the case. The blind rigidity of economics has not been duplicated. Strategy is more fluid. There is room for companies to achieve competitive advantage, to alter the balance of power within industries, and – over time – to diversify successfully into closely connected businesses. Yet the underlying assumption of industry stability has only been modified, not abandoned. The predominant management philosophy still depends on relatively stable industries.

Two of the most influential works in the area of strategic management echo a similar theme of internally generated growth. The best seller by Peters and Waterman, *In Search of Excellence*, stresses that companies should "stick to their knitting."[3] Firms do best when they stay close to what they know. Since its publication, however, events have forced some changes in the tone of this book. A number of companies identified as "excellent" in the book subsequently reported below-average performances. Unforeseen events upset the authors' simplistic rules for success. Being pragmatic, both authors in separate follow-on works elaborate slightly altered versions of the original formula. Emphasis shifts to the inherent uncertainties, and chaotic nature, of doing business. The new message alerts firms to be prepared to weather inevitable storms. Only those firms adapting to new threats and seizing new opportunities will survive. In the midst of this turmoil, neither Peters nor Waterman deviate from a preoccupation with business-level strategy. Every division and every business must strive to reduce costs, to raise productivity, and, in general, to learn to operate with fewer and more efficient employees. Cases and key points provide helpful examples. The basic theme translates into attention to basics; to get better at the same things. Almost no guidelines are volunteered for corporate-level strategy: that is, to examine whether companies might do better by doing different things. In view of the unprecedented and almost continuous activity in mergers and acquisitions as well as corporate restructurings since the 1950s, this seems a peculiar oversight. Hundreds of companies have taken steps to change their basic characters, adding new businesses, divesting old ones, and moving from one industry to another. In sum, Peters' and Waterman's advice, though sound and effectively communicated, was aimed at business unit managers. No advice was given to chief executives of multi-business or multidivisional firms on how best to manage the mix of different operations. Despite a concern for change, they expressed no awareness of the type of change that was occurring around them. While entire corporations were being restructured, Peters' and Waterman's attention was riveted on the individual business units rather than the overall firm.

Michael Porter of Harvard University has also published best-selling books on strategic management. Perhaps no single academic has had a greater impact on the professional study of this field. His two major works – *Competitive Strategy* and *Competitive Advantage* – address the appropriate range of strategies for a firm's corporate as well as business level.[4] The book on business-level strategy was the first and the most influential of the two. While endorsing Peters' and Waterman's general thrust for excellence at the business level, Porter's treatment was considerably more systematic and scholarly. The foundation for Porter's exposition drew heavily on industrial organization economics, a branch of mainstream economics pioneered by Edward Mason in the 1930s and Joseph Bain in the 1950s.[5] This special framework for competition has not changed in its fundamental assumptions since then. Basically, markets determine firm performance. At the center of industrial organization economics is the structure of markets, which determines conduct and performance. In the traditional structure–conduct–performance relationship, firm performance in terms of profitability, efficiency, etc. depends on the conduct of buyers and sellers. Conduct, in turn, is shaped by the structure of markets, as reflected by the number and size of firms, the difficulty of entry by new firms, and general conditions for competitiveness within each relevant market or industry.

Industrial organization economics was originally developed in order to aid government regulators select antitrust policies that could force prices down to minimum levels, primarily by lowering barriers to entry and competition. Porter reformulated industrial organization economics as a positive force for firms to gain competitive advantage within their industries. To do so, firms needed to modify structural characteristics of markets in their favor, either by creating high barriers to entry, or by reducing the number of industry competitors, or by increasing product differentiation, or by affecting demand for their products and services. The accomplishment of one or more of these goals formed the basis for making a difference in terms of competitive strategy.

This reinterpretation by Porter contravened the initial application of industrial organization economics as a means for assuring minimum corporate profits for firms and therefore implicitly minimizing the role of corporate strategy. Furthermore, a key assumption of industrial organization economics was that market structure was "definitionally stable."[6] Porter relaxed, but did not abandon this condition. He invented tactical maneuvers like "mobility barriers" (which discourage shifts among competitors within industries) and "exit barriers" (which tend to keep competitors locked into an industry); these maneuvers implied structural stability and perceived dynamism primarily through intra-industry rivalry.

In his corollary work on corporate strategy, a condition of relatively stable industry structures was maintained.[7] This stability is fundamental to Porter's analysis of corporate-level strategy. Assuming relative stability, companies cannot deviate from their assigned industries in the short run. Over time, industries evolve, according to Porter, but only if companies can transfer skills or share activities in new industries. By definition, therefore, a company is destined to remain within its industry or diversify only into related industries that are tied into an existing skill or are exploiting an underutilized resource of the diversifying firm. Unrelated diversification, though not definitionally excluded, is ruled out because no crossover of skills or sharing of common activities pertain.

A key factor in deciding which diversification moves qualify as "good" or "bad" relies on Porter's so-called "value chain." The value chain consists of a primary set of activities – actions necessary to, say, build a product, market it, and service it – plus secondary and supporting activities like human resource management, technology, and procurement. These activities are the basis for common bonds between businesses, as when expertise in marketing one type of consumer goods can be transferred and used as a basis for developing or acquiring a new product line of consumer goods requiring similar marketing expertise. Similarly, the value chain can identify situations when sharing of activities makes sense, as in the instance of two business units sharing the same sales force.

Transferring skills and sharing activities produce gain, if combining activities reduces costs. The emphasis on costs is not accidental. Cost reduction is the economist's only route to raising a firm's performance. In traditional economics, the assumption of strong competition within stable market structures leads inexorably to pressure on prices and an implied firm strategy of becoming the low-cost producer. In a business-level sense, this has application, and every business unit should strive to squeeze out excess costs and eliminate redundant activities. Once these tasks are addressed, however, the overall question remains of whether the corporation is in the right businesses. This is not addressed by Porter's analysis.

Porter's prescription for corporate-level strategy is essentially an extension of his business-level philosophy, which in turn derives from the static structural model of industrial organization economics. Porter builds his version of business- and corporate-level strategy without apparent reliance on the history of how modern businesses evolved or appreciation for the motivations that drove firms to adapt and change. Ignoring firm experiences and the motivations behind them freed Porter from the complications of explaining all the exceptions to his frameworks for business and corporate strategy. Companies like General Electric, United States Steel (USX), Procter & Gamble, Sears, and American Express – to mention just a few of the major diversified giants – participate in more than one major industry, but did not achieve that spread by implementing Porter's value-chain concept. In fact, the scant evidence available suggests that the idea of shared activities, in particular, works better in theory than in practice, as the following quote by Walter Kiechel III, an editor for *Fortune* magazine, illustrates:

> Actually, this concept [of shared costs] had initially been thought up by George Bennet and others when they were at BCG working on a case at Texas Instruments. So I went back to Texas Instruments, where the idea originated, to ask, "How do you use the share cost idea?" They said, "It was a little too complicated for our line managers. We didn't use it."[8]

Transferring skills into another company as a means of improving the prospect for successful diversification outcomes is a strategy I have endorsed in my book *Managing the Unmanageable*.[9] The difference is that I was considering diversification into new industries or new businesses. As an example, Raytheon acquired Amana, an appliance maker, in 1965. Raytheon used its expertise in defense electronics to develop the first microwave oven, and then transferred the technology to Amana, thus enabling the latter to dominate microwave sales for a decade. This transference of expertise from defense electronics in order to develop a market advantage in home appliances offers one example of how two basically unrelated businesses might benefit from an infusion of a particular skill from one to the other. I give other examples in my book of corporations transferring skills as a basis for maximizing their performance in *different* businesses. My basis for defining different types of diversification depends on a tradititional distinction between different lines of business: that is, a company operating in two clearly dissimilar businesses, like defense electronics and home appliances, represents unrelated diversification. Michael Porter, on the other hand, avoids making a distinction according to the many ways in which companies in two industries differ. Instead, he introduces a singular and ambiguous new concept that perceives two merging companies that share *any* common elements in terms of their value chains as being *potentially* related (a topic that will be picked up again later).

Overall, Porter plays down the difficulty of making his dual concepts of skill transference and cost sharing work, and the time taken to make them effective, while ignoring the potential for *any* advantage from trying a strategy of less related or unrelated diversification. Portfolio-type diversification, for example, is derided as "no way to conduct corporate strategy."[10] As a permanent strategy this may be true, as Alfred Chandler observed from his careful review of how big businesses grew and prospered. Yet portfolio-type diversification is generally a *first step* in a long process of integrating and managing a mix of businesses. Conglomerates formed in the 1960s provided classic examples of how not to diversify. Many hastily contrived empires came unstuck in the next decade. The failure of conglomerates to perform effectively was not because they lacked common skills or activities, however, but because they failed to formulate and then implement a clear long-run strategy. Many individual conglomerates were destined to underperform, and some deserved to fail. Random acquiring still persists and some of these cases will probably be added to the list of conglomerate "casualties" and thereby reinforce the belief that companies should "stick to their knitting."

Individual instances of failure by diversified firms add fuel to the theoretical proposition of relative industry stability; a claim, by the way, that completely lacks empirical support. Indeed, the historical record compiled by Alfred Chandler and extended to the present time argues just the opposite. The data support a Schumpeterian style of growth, punctuated by explosive periods of change rather than slow evolutionary adaptation. A number of industrial revolutions since the middle of the nineteenth century, the approximate date for the beginnings of modern capitalism, sustain Schumpeter's thesis. Initially, firms moved to rationalize their operations through a series of vertical and horizontal combinations. Around the turn of the century, major consolidations among competing firms formed the nucleus of such giant corporations as American Can, International Paper, National Dairy, United States Steel, General Electric, and American Tobacco. Corporations used acquisitions to integrate vertically during the 1920s, while also diversifying internally by exploiting research and development skills in related markets and products. The conglomerate phase, from the mid-1950s to the mid-1960s, was characterized by the building of wide-ranging enterprises of unrelated businesses; this was followed by a period of divestment and revaluation of strategy. Finally, the 1980s ushered in an era of novel and drastic restructurings through unfriendly takeovers, leveraged buyouts, divestitures, and refinancings.

The periodic reshuffling of the industrial landscape hardly meets the criterion of stability. Underneath, a consistent drive for growth and market power has always worked to change the shape of business capitalism: a trend that is as vital and perpetual as ever.

For a closer inspection of change, a statistical portrait is helpful. Table 2.1, for example, looks at stability in terms of staying power experienced by the top fifty industrial companies as ranked in 1909. Only seven companies – Exxon, General Electric, DuPont, American Brands, International Paper, United States Steel, and Westinghouse – were counted among the top fifty industrial firms by 1987. Of these, only Exxon, and to a lesser degree International Paper, are true examples of stability. General Electric, American Brands, and Westinghouse are conglomerates in character, although that appellation is so tainted that no company willingly describes itself as such. United States Steel is no longer classified in the steel industry because two-thirds of its revenues come from oil and gas. DuPont, by acquiring Continental Oil, also has a significant participation in the energy business. Roughly two-thirds of the names in the list of companies in table 2.1 have either been liquidated or acquired.

In a similar survey, *Forbes* magazine chronicled the dropout rate between 1917 and 1987 among the hundred largest companies in 1917. Only 22 survived. Of the other 78, some grew, "but not fast enough to stay on the list . . . plenty of what were viewed as blue chips 70 years ago simply deceased as companies, although some assets may remain."[11]

This dismal record on the persistence of big companies is paralleled when making comparisons according to industry rankings between 1917 and 1987. In table 2.2, oil is the exceptional case of a stable industry, moving up from a number 2 position to number 1. The biggest industry of all in 1917 – steel – failed to make the list in 1987. Indeed, half of the industries that appeared among the top industries in 1917 failed the test of time. Moving up to replace them were new industries: computers, aerospace, pharmaceuticals, scientific and photographic equipment, among others. Just as individual companies change their "character," so too do industries. By whatever measure, the data support Schumpeter's case for chronic instability better than an argument for industry stability.

But what about inter-industry diversification? Could these shifts conceivably be explained by companies moving within industries and industries adjusting relative to one another? Again, the opposite seems to be the

Table 2.1 Disposition of the fifty largest industrials in 1909 (ranked according to size of assets)

Rank in 1909	Company	No longer independent	Still independent (name change)	Rank in 1987
1	US Steel		(USX, mostly oil)	16
2	Standard Oil of NJ		(Exxon)	2
3	American Tobacco		(American Brands)	49
4	International Harvester		(Navistar)	182
5	Amalgamated Copper	acquired by ARCO, 1977		
6	Central Leather	liquidated, 1953		
7	Pullman	acquired by Wheelabrator Frye, 1980		
8	Armour	acquired by General Host, 1969		
9	American Sugar		(Amstar, private company)	
10	US Rubber	in liquidation, 1986		
11	American Smelting and Refining		(Asarco)	167
12	Singer Manufacturing	acquired by private investor, 1988		
13	Swift	fresh meat operations continue as an independent company	(Swift International)	
14	Pittsburgh Coal	acquired by Consolidated Coal, 1966		
15	General Electric		same	6
16	American Car & Foundary		(ACF, private company)	
17	Colorado Fuel & Iron	acquired by Crane, 1969		
18	Corn Products	acquired by Philip Morris, 1985		
19	American Can	can factories acquired by Triangle Ind., 1986		

Table 2.1 (cont.)   Disposition of the fifty largest industrials in 1909 (ranked according to size of assets)

Rank in 1909	Company	No longer independent	Still independent (name change)	Rank in 1987
20	Lacakawanna	acquired by Bethlehem Steel, 1923		
21	American Woolens	acquired by Textron, 1955		
22	Westinghouse		same	33
23	Consolidated Coal	acquired by Continental Oil, 1967		
24	DuPont		same	10
25	Republic Steel	merge with LTV, 1984		
26	Va-Carolina Chemical	acquired by Mobil, 1962		
27	International Paper		same	37
28	Bethlehem Steel		same	74
29	American Locomotive	acquired by Worthington, 1964		
30	National Biscuit	merged with Standard Brands, 1981		
31	Cambria Steel	acquired by Midvale Steel, 1916		
32	Chile Copper	acquired by Anaconda, 1923		
33	Distillers Securities		(Quantum Chemicals)	146
34	Calumet & Hecia	acquired by UOP, 1968		
35	American Agricultural Chemical	acquired by Continental Oil, 1963		
36	Allis-Chalmers		same	438
37	Crucible Steel	acquired by Colt Industries, 1963		
38	Lake Superior	unknown end		
39	US Smelting & Refining	in liquidation, 1979		
40	United Copper	liquidated, 1913		
41	National Lead	majority interest Vallie, 1986		

Rank in 1909	Company	No longer independent	Still independent (name change)	Rank in 1987
42	Phelps Dodge		same	159
43	Lehigh Coal	liquidated, 1965		
44	International Steam Pump	liquidated, 1915		
45	Jones & Laughlin	acquired by LTV, 1974		
46	Western Electric	part of AT&T		
47	Associated Oil	acquired by Tidewater Assoc. Oil, 1926		
48	American Writing Paper	liquidated, 1962		
49	Copper Range	unknown end		
50	United Fruit	majority interest owned by American Financial		

Source: Milton Leontiades, *Managing the Unmanageable* (Addison-Wesley, Reading, Mass., 1986), pp. 30–2, as revised.

case. From the mid-1950s, the conglomerate "wave" of activity carried many firms away from core businesses. During the following decades, many companies were either voluntarily divesting their mistakes or forced as a result of takeovers to restructure, refocus, or liquidate.

Yet the failings of some conglomerates hardly tell the whole story. Many very diversified companies still operate successfully: for example, General Electric, United Technologies, Textron, Gulf and Western, Westinghouse, Teledyne, American Brands, and Food Machinery and Chemical (FMC), to name a few. Relative newcomers to a strategy of diversification have, by their actions, shown a commitment to lessen their reliance on a single industry: for example, Procter & Gamble, Sears, Kodak, Philip Morris, Ralston Purina, and others. Still other companies have either left or sharply curtailed the percentage of revenues generated by original lines of business, a strategy contrary to the advice for companies to "stick to their knitting." Westinghouse sold its light bulb and major appliance businesses; Singer transformed itself from a sewing machine manufacturer to a diversified aerospace company (only to be taken over and largely dismembered); Insilco jettisoned the silverware line; Greyhound is no longer a bus company; Union Carbide no longer makes batteries. An entire industry – rubber tires – has practically been vacated; much of the productive capacity has been sold to foreign companies (only Goodyear remains as a major domestic producer of rubber tires).

Table 2.2   Industry ranking by assets

Industry	1917–1987		1987	Industry
Steel	1	—[a]	1	Petroleum refining
Oil	2	1	2	Electronics
Copper and nickel	3	—[a]	3	Motor vehicle parts
Meat-packing.	4	—	4	Chemicals
Electrical equipment	5	2	5	Computers
Chemicals	6	4	6	Food
Shipping	7	—	7	Aerospace
Automobiles	8	3	8	Forest products
Rubber	9	19	9	Pharmaceuticals
Miscellaneous	10	—	10	Metals
Rail equipment	11	25	11	Scientific and photographic equipment
Tobacco	12	13	12	Industrial and farm equipment
Farm equipment	13	12	13	Tobacco
Coal	14	—	14	Beverages
Merchandizing	15	22	15	Publishing and printing
Food	16	6	16	Building materials
Sugar	17	—	17	Soaps, cosmetics
Textiles	18	21	18	Metal products
Aluminum	19	—[a]	19	Rubber products
Paper	20	8	20	Mining, crude oil production

[a] Not strictly comparable. In 1987, "steel" includes aluminum, steel, copper, and nickel. The United States Steel Company, the largest company in 1917, is classified in the "oil" industry in 1987 as a result of acquiring Marathon Oil and Texas Oil and Gas.
Sources: Data for 1917 are based on estimates of assets for the top 100 companies, *Forbes*, September 15, 1967, p. 76. Data for 1987 are based on estimates of assets for the top 500 companies, *Fortune*, April 25, 1988, p. D58.

What motivations underlie the frenzied activity to diversify and change? Few have bothered to ask. No current theory of diversification exists that incorporates the motivations of those who control corporate America. Yet without discerning who controls, and their underlying motivations, any explanation remains partial at best. What at present passes for an explanation in strategic management draws a considerable part of its justification from a branch of economics (industrial organization economics) that was developed with a static market structure in mind. As adapted by Michael Porter, industrial organization economics was modified, but structural stability and an orientation on the business level were kept largely intact. Porter failed to elevate his analysis to the corporate level effectively, because of his belief that "diversified companies do not compete; only their business units do."[12]

This is an extraordinary statement for Porter to make in view of all the observable inconsistencies. As an example, since Jack Welch became chief executive officer in 1981, General Electric sold over 200 businesses, spent $11 billion to buy 300 new ones, closed 73 facilities, and reduced employment by two-thirds.[13] David Broderick, chairman of United States Steel, has stated unequivocally that his company will *not* be used to reinvest solely in the present businesses: "There's just no question. This is going to be a cash cow . . . [to] do a lot of things – buy back stock, make acquisitions or reduce debt."[14]

Clearly, such decisions rise above business-level responsibilities. They typify actions that do not fit well within Porter's framework. Equally transparent is the fact that such corporate-level decisions will dictate the success or failure of the entire corporation on which the health of the individual business units depend. Further, such strategies do not – as Porter claims – "grow out of" the collective business strategies. Business unit managers can and should be given authority for diversification that builds on established expertise, skills, or technology, and meets Porter's guideline of constrained expansion. On the other hand, the most strategic moves – those that influence the survival of the firm and include major acquisitions in new industries and divestments of old businesses – cannot be dealt with at the business level. Only an independent, all-inclusive view from the top can develop strategy for the entire organization. Thus far, this compelling logic has not garnered nearly the attention it deserves. While economists and business strategists alike have dwelled on developing a rationale for optimizing the business level, top corporate executives have been desperately trying to maximize the performance of the total organization.

Clues to a more comprehensive explanation of the facts exist, but have largely been overlooked. Schumpeter's notion of dynamic disequilibrium, for example, is at the other pole from traditional views in mainstream economics as well as those of industrial organization economics. Schumpeter posits the central problem in economics as structural instability rather than structural immobility. But innovation and entrepreneurship, both necessary to Schumpeter's perspective, cannot be managed within economic models of static equilibrium or industrial organization frameworks of structural stability.

Edith Penrose, another economist, holds to a theory of diversification limited only by managerial resources to control it.[15] Her theory implies that diversification is a normal part of management's strategic arsenal and not merely a reaction to market conditions.

Both Schumpeter's and Penrose's explanations fit the facts better than current doctrine. Unfortunately, however, the views of Schumpeter and Penrose have not been heeded. Theories more amenable to mainstream doctrine prevail, while conflicting views are denied serious consideration.

A tendency to favor only those facts that fit – rather than constructing a theory to fit the facts – is a general concern for management. As a case in point, the emphasis within strategic management on the business level clearly deserves re-examination. This focus does not fulfill the mission of higher education in business that the authors of the Carnegie and Ford Foundation studies had in mind when they suggested a course to study the firm as a whole and from the top. As a profession, management still has not come to grips with the corporate brain, the nerve center that controls all of the extremities. How top managers optimize strategy for the entire firm, especially the strategy of diversification, remains an unexamined puzzle of management research, limiting the ability of the profession to enlighten, or even understand, management practices. In particular, the normal assumption of relative industry stability needs to be revised in order to keep step with modern management actions and thinking.

Myth 2: Capital for Business Investment is Allocated by the Market

Efficiently operating markets are at the heart of economic theory, with the capital market, in particular, being fundamental to modern finance theory as well. The capital market as visualized involves active bidding between large numbers of suppliers and users of funds. Capital allocation is governed by what Adam Smith referred to as the invisible hand of the market system. Neither businesses nor individual investors are deemed powerful enough to influence the sheer force of collective market decisions. Using a metaphor descriptive of that type of environment, one observer likened firms to "islands of conscious power in this ocean of unconscious cooperation, like lumps of butter coagulating in a pail of buttermilk."[16]

Modern business enterprise, however, is no longer faceless or powerless. Nor is it totally dependent on the capital market to supply it with investment capital. The so-called "lumps" of insignificance have transformed into very significant sources of capital in their own right. In many respects, the modern business firm has replaced the market as the principal allocative mechanism. As firms grow, so does the amount of cash they are able to generate internally. Initially, as product-markets continue to expand, the demand for expansion capital exceeds what can be met from a firm's own resources. But as businesses mature and markets move toward saturation, the relative level of investment outlays tends to moderate, while the ability for self-financing tends to increase. A combination of slowing growth in product-markets and rising internal cash flows increasingly allows companies to divorce themselves from dependence on outside equity and, to a lesser extent, debt financing. For companies that are wholly or mainly self-sustaining, the judgment of corporate managers substitutes for the decision-making process of the capital market.

An abundance of statistical evidence suggests that big business is generally able to operate with minimum reliance on the capital market, especially for new issues of common stock, the "risk capital" deemed so basic to a capitalistic system. In one study, an aggregate of $150 billion was estimated to have been spent on capital expenditures in the United States from 1946 to 1953. Of that sum, 64 percent came from internal sources – retained earnings plus depreciation, depletion, and amortization of debt – and another 30 percent was accounted for by short-term borrowings or the issuance of corporate debt. Only 6 percent was raised by the sale of stock, with an undetermined, but significant portion of that amount represented by preferred rather than common stock.[17]

Another, more recent study of equity financing by half of the *Fortune 500* companies from 1940 to 1978 substantiated the scant supplies of risk capital provided by the capital market. Of the 250 firms surveyed, "only 27% . . . sold common stock for internal financing purposes (other than when initially going public) and only 8% had more than one equity offering during these 38 years."[18]

While the supply and demand for investment capital has increasingly come to be resolved internally through decisions of fewer and larger corporations, the profile of the typical equity investor has also radically altered. Large institutions – pension funds, mutual funds, insurance companies, banks, and brokerage firms – dominate trading activity in the stock market. Professional managers of other peoples' money have taken the place of legions of small individual investors. These institutional money managers control and invest huge sums in order to meet future pension obligations, as overseers of personal trust accounts, as a means for diversifying small investment accounts, etc. Pension-fund managers, especially, benefit from a large and continuous inflow of funds periodically paid by business and other organizations to fulfill their pension-plan obligations.

With the growth in the amount of money to be invested has come a concomitant growth in the size of professional management firms, in order to achieve the economies of large scale and thus provide the level of services and advice demanded by their clients. By one informed estimate, stock market action has come to be dominated mainly by only 2,200 active traders, with even fewer traders – between 150 and 200 so-called "lead steers" – who are really important.[19] Unfortunately, reliable and up-to-date statistics on the composition and characteristics of stock investors are hard to come by. What is known for sure is that large institutions have steadily displaced the small investor.

1 In a 1985 study by the New York Stock Exchange (NYSE), only 20 percent of the public directly held stock or stock mutual funds, and only 1–3 percent of those were "big" investors whose holdings exceeded $50,000.[20] By comparison, institutions loom gigantic, especially in terms of the percentage of the total value of stock traded in the capital market.

2 The two largest traders of NYSE stock at the end of 1985 were pension funds (57 percent of total) and mutual funds (15 percent of total). The turnover of stock by these two institutions was 80 percent and 100 percent respectively.[21]

3 Pension funds alone now own 25 percent, by value, of all corporate shares traded in the United States and that figure is expected to keep growing.[22]

4 Pension funds have assets exceeding $1.8 trillion, roughly thirteen times the total two decades ago. By the year 2000, assets are estimated to reach $3.5 trillion. If the share of pension-fund assets held in common stocks remains at the current 40 percent, these funds could own 50 percent of all corporate equity.[23]

5 The turnover of outstanding shares has more than tripled, from 20.1 percent in 1977 to 72.4 percent in 1987 – the highest level since 1929 – with pension funds and brokerage firms accounting for nearly three-quarters of all NYSE volume.[24]

The enormous trading activity concentrated in a relatively few institutions – coupled with a sharp decline in the demand for equity capital by business – leads to an inescapable conclusion that something other than traditional financing is taking place. What has developed, in fact, is the creation of two markets, one for trading in outstanding securities and another for financing new investment by American business. Of the two functions, trading, including speculation, attracts the talents of the biggest and best capitalized players. Far from being anonymous and powerless, institutions are very visible and influential in the capital market; none the less, their size and actions cannot be explained in terms of their providing equity financing to emerging new ventures or for the plant and equipment expenditures of existing businesses. To the degree that insititutional investors do not use the capital market for "productive" investments, nor do corporations rely on external equity capital, the underlying justification of the stock market in terms of assuring allocative efficiency is stripped away.

Structural changes in the last half century have "hollowed out" the capital market. The edifice is standing, but the action has shifted elsewhere. The norm of small mercantilist firms and individual risk-takers has been superseded by big businesses and big institutional investors. Large mature corporations expose themselves only intermittently and in limited degree to the market's influence. Professional investment companies, on the other hand, trade securities among themselves, but do not – except for occasional purchases of new common stock issues – directly supply risk capital to America's corporations. These dramatic changes have not visibly impressed theorists, who still maintain the essential elements of the classical market system. In this regard, finance theory is indistinguishable from economic theory, so whatever virtue or failing may be true of economics is likewise applicable to the financial aspects of strategic management.

The means by which economic theory remains connected to practice is through the principle known as "opportunity costs," which assigns a cost to funds used for investment whether obtained through the capital market or not. Although no out-of-pocket expense is associated with the use of a company's internal funds, opportunity cost in principle precludes a firm from reinvesting funds, unless the return promises to exceed the returns that shareholders could realize from investing the money on their own. The effect is to view all funds as bearing a cost comparable to the actual cost the market would have set. This "opportunity cost of funds" represents a theoretical "hurdle rate of return on investments" that companies must overcome in order to justify reinvesting the funds generated from operations.

Strict adherence to the opportunity-cost principle makes actual reliance on the capital markets immaterial. Trips to and from the market can be simulated, creating a convergence between theory and managerial actions. However, what makes an impression on theorists does not necessarily motivate business managers. If managers were truly indifferent between internal and external funds, there would be much greater willingness to raise equity capital and a much better balance in the way typical companies are capitalized. If the purpose of theory is to prepare managers better for practice, there must be empirical linkages connecting the hypothetical and descriptive cases.

Radical restructurings on both the demand and supply sides of the capital market suggest a recasting of a theory that in essence is more than 200 years old. To assert that the actions of modern managers who control large pools of internally generated capital have the same influence today as the typically small merchant firm proprietor of yesteryear acting in an atomistic market is an implausible supposition. Might not the values of managers in large corporations be influenced by organizational pressures and self-interests different from those a dispassionate market would dictate? And would not the motivations of corporate managers probably differ from the interests of investors? When asked, managers do indeed seem to be swayed by considerations other than those contained in the theorist's frame of reference. Whereas normative theory assumes that managers openly and objectively evaluate investments in relation to an implied cost of capital, many managers in practice seek to minimize their use of external financing, thus freeing themselves from the market's discipline. Moreover, contrary to popular theory, diversification through acquisitions in many companies tends to be thought of as an essential part of good strategy by business managers, even though the financing of acquisitions is seldom decided in the marketplace by the votes of equity investors, and the act of diversification runs counter to the theoretical imperative of specialization. Acquiring new businesses generally reflects top management's "clear recognition of the organizational vulnerability created by excessive dependence on single products, markets, or technology: such choices seek to assure that the corporation will survive even as industries mature and die."[25]

These feelings expressed by managers seem eminently sensible. The fact that survival of the company serves the interests of managers seems transparent and the impact of self-interest on individual motivation goes back to Adam Smith himself. Managerial decisions contrary to those the market might dictate do not imply irrationality of either managers or markets, merely a difference. In both cases, capital allocation is efficiently allocated. Firms locked in competition with one another are hardly indifferent to investment outcomes that will determine survivors and also-rans. No company or manager can afford to dissipate funds indefinitely, whether those funds come from internal or external sources, without losing ground to competitors and risking the personal consequences. Competition by itself is a powerful force to assure efficiency in the use of all of a company's resources, including capital. The important question is not whether firms strive for efficiency as a general objective – which is an unarguable position in principle – but the way the goal is defined and the means for its achievement.

Initial abstractions of the investment process by theorists may be a necessary first step as a way to simplify the analysis of a complex problem. Subsequent checks by objective analysis should serve to confirm or deny the validity of the first approximations. Unfortunately, it is tempting to stick with the abstraction and treat deviations from it as irrational. Using the case in point, the rise of modern capitalism permanently displaced the larger part of the market's role in supplying equity for business expansion. Yet the effect of these dislocations on firm behavior, and the readjustments to the definition of capital-market efficiency that are implied, are still to be studied seriously or incorporated into new theory.

An argument has been advanced that diversified firms may be better allocators of capital than the market.[26] Whether or not that is so, managers may properly evaluate diversification from a different perspective than than of the market, while viewing specialization as a limiting form of strategy. For a company with a large market share in a mature industry, for example, the chances are that it is generating more cash than it can profitably reinvest – the proverbial cash cow. At this stage, cash flows can be considered as "surplus," if the company is inflexibly committed to remain in a single industry, or they can be invested in related or unrelated businesses that appear to promise a satisfactory rate of return. Theory says the shareholders should get the cash. Managers have preferred to diversify. If one accepts survival and growth as motivating factors for management, diversification is a viable and explainable option. If, however, industry specialization is an unconditional part of theory, diversion of funds to shareholders is an inescapable conclusion. Whatever answer is reached depends on the conditions assumed: those from a model based on a theorist's untested hypothesis or those incorporating the actions and motivations of actual business managers.

In practical terms, every company has access to its own funds and to that extent it is a supplier of its own capital. The expenditure of those funds is at the discretion of managements, who may decide that diversification is the best available course to assure the future prosperity of the company. The result of the decision may not always coincide with what the company's investors would prefer – assuming that a collective judgment could be reached – but that does not make the decision irrational or the strategy inappropriate. Before that judgment can be reached, the basis for managerial actions must be understood – a step that cannot be achieved by staying within the confines of a theory where cause and effect are predetermined.

Myth 3: Maximizing Shareholder Wealth is the Test of Good Management

Maximizing shareholder wealth is a tenet of finance and economics that has also become a slogan of big business. Everyone, it seems, considers wealth creation for shareholders as a desirable goal. Since stock prices reflect the value of a shareholder's investment in a firm, the benchmark of good management is the ability to raise the price of the firm's common shares. On the surface, an ideal joining of theory and practice at last seems possible.

Alas, on close inspection, the consensus is more apparent than real. What management has in mind by an increase in shareholder value is a *long-term* enhancement of firm efficiency that will work to the betterment of all its *stakeholders*, including customers, suppliers, employees, and society in general. Finance makes no distinction between the short and long term, nor does it recognize the claims of any stakeholders other than owners of shares in the firm. Stock price is the only measure of value *at any time*, and whoever owns the common stock of the firm is the one to be rewarded, regardless of all other contingencies.

This simple one-directional transfer of gains to shareholders would equally promote the interests of a mixed collection of shareholders with differing investment objectives, including institutions, traders, arbitrageurs, widows and orphans, corporate investors, foreign investors, and whoever else happened to own a piece of American business. By virtue of their legal claims of ownership, shareholders are viewed as interchangeable and are all entitled to due diligence by management to work totally on their behalf. The tight link between ownership and rewards derives from the enduring portrait of the typical business sketched by Adam Smith. Drawing on the business environment he observed, Smith depicted a community of small firms where the owners were also the managers. In this situation, the single owner–manager had a personal interest to further and would naturally work hard to maximize profits, since he would reap the rewards from his own labor. It would be equally logical, Smith perceived, that hired managers left on their own would have different interests from the owner, and also that outside financiers might not share the owner's interests.[27]

As late as 1840, Adam Smith's original concepts prevailed, with nearly all top managers also still serving as owners. Within a century, however, the tasks of management and ownership were split; professional managers assumed control of operations and ownership became disbursed among many individual and institutional investors with no personal ties to business. Berle and Means, in their classic *The Modern Corporation and Private Property*, meticulously documented this new arrangement between managers and owners.[28] As subsequently confirmed by events, the separation proved permanent and irreversible. As a consequence, the business conditions defined by Adam Smith changed in two fundamental ways: managers no longer had a significant financial stake in the firms they managed, and shareowners no longer had a long-term personal commitment to the firms in which they invested.

Today's managers are far removed from yesterday's entrepreneurial capitalists in very practical ways. They do not risk their own funds. Should the firm fare poorly, a manager might lose his job, but not his capital. Similarly, the new owners are owners in a legal sense only. They shoulder neither the manager's responsibility of managing, nor the owner's risk of unlimited liability. Dividends and price appreciation hold out the promise of unlimited gains to shareowners, but, in the event of ill fortune or even the demise of the firm, shareowners stand to lose only the amounts invested. Despite the distancing of owners from firms, the legal right of organizational control and the implied risks thereof form the present-day basis for shareowners to hold a pre-emptive claim on firm profits.[29] Yet the implication of shareholder control or shareholder risk is at odds with the average stockholder's changed position as a passive investor rather than an owner/risk-taker. Typically, modern investors do not seek involvement or responsibility. On average, the typical individual shareowner does not attend annual meetings when invited. He or she does not vote proxies when solicited. Brokerage houses or other financial intermediaries often hold the common shares of individual investors and receive the communications issued by companies. In every way, individual investors avoid any type of ownership commitment and make it unmistakably clear that the purchase of stock is simply for investment. Even large institutions with sizeable stakes in companies, which would entitle their voices to be heard, generally interpret their legal rights narrowly and are moved to action only under extraordinary circumstances. Moreover, the shareowners' legal right to control is extremely tenuous. By statute, management control is reserved to the board of directors, who are not agents of stockholders and are not required to follow stockholders' instructions. In every statute in the country, the board's power and duty to manage and supervise is abundantly clear. The fact that stockholders lack this authority is equally apparent.[30]

A second transformation since small businesses were in vogue is the short-term orientation of modern investors. Old-fashioned owner–managers had their life savings in the business and watched those savings very carefully. They worked extremely hard to preserve and add to their capital. By virtue of "sweat equity," these sturdy pioneers built American industry to a pre-eminent place in world trade. Since owner's jobs as well as their capital was sunk into the business, the tenure of ownership usually meant a lifetime attachment, extending to the founder's heirs, who generally continued to have a working interest in the business.

Current owners no longer have close personal ties with the businesses in which they invest, nor the long-term perspective and rationale of a founder or succeeding generations of family managers and owners. Ownership today reflects the policies and attitudes of the large institutions that have come to dominate the capital market. The shift is from a very long-term to an extremely short-term orientation. Institutions hold no attachment to the shares they so frequently buy and sell. Investment managers often commit or withdraw funds from the market according to formula so that individual companies are not even identified. Sophisticated computer-activated buy and sell programs do not need a personal involvement by fund managers. This emotionless attitude to investments is reinforced by pressures for short-term results. Forced to reveal quarter-by-quarter results, fund managers have little choice but to tend to the near term. Nor do fund managers have total freedom in making decisions to sell stocks they own, when faced with offers to buy. A fiduciary responsibility to their own investors or clients gives them neither the flexibility nor personal choice common to individual shareowners. If holdings are sold, the institutions generally take the proceeds and reinvest in new investment opportunities. In sum, the motivation and commitment of institutions could hardly contrast more starkly with the "full-blooded capitalist" of a prior era, as Schumpeter succinctly phrased it. While the pioneering owner of yore stood ready to fight for his property, the security owner of the twentieth century has only the vaguest idea what property it is that he or she owns or where it is located.

How might the United States have fared if the founders of major corporations had only the short term in mind? An example of one respected company , Procter & Gamble, serves as a useful reminder of the foresight that made America an industrial powerhouse. Founded in 1837, Procter & Gamble is older than 99 percent of domestic companies. When Cooper Procter, the firm's chief executive, implemented a plan early in the 1920s to sell directly to retailers, it was thought a risky and revolutionary idea. Resistance from wholesalers plus an economic recession resulted in a one-year loss of over $30 million, an amount roughly equal to what the company had earned in the previous five years. Although Cooper Procter knew this would drive down the price of the company's stock in the short run, he confidently wrote: "My own judgment and prestige will suffer . . . I cannot help it . . . In the long run, the present plan will work for the advantage of the average stockholder who held his stock as an investment and not as a speculation."[31]

Cooper Procter's prophecy proved to be accurate and Procter & Gamble as a result strengthened its competitiveness. But could a chief executive afford to fix so single-mindedly on the long run today? With the swing toward the institutional investor and a concomitant emphasis on short-term results, managers no longer exercise the same degree of control, nor do they view temporary downswings in their firm's share price with the same confidence.

Over fifty years ago, Adolph Berle and Gardiner Means recognized the consequence that separation of ownership and control would have on managerial prerogatives, but the full potential of their argument did not materialize until relatively recently. Not until the 1980s was the right of management to exercise control actively contested. Until that time, a benign contract between shareholders and firms gave almost complete freedom of control to managers. As long as shareholders remained uninvolved, managers were *de facto* in charge. However, the era of hostile takeovers and corporate restructurings in the 1980s destroyed the illusion of calm. The neutrality of shareowners was seized upon by financial entrepreneurs on the prowl for firms whose assets were undervalued by the market. By offering to buy out shareowners at prices above current market quotes, opportunists like T. Boone Pickens, Carl Icahn, Asher Edelman, Irwin Jacobs, Saul Steinberg, and Sir James Goldsmith changed the face of industrial America.

The buying and selling of companies is not new of course. Since well before the turn of the century, companies have been buying other firms in an effort to create more efficient organizations. Recent takeover activity differs from the past in one very important respect: control no longer carries with it the responsibility of managing. Financial entrepreneurs with few exceptions express no interest in managing or creating operating efficiencies. Their commitment is only for the short term – often a matter of weeks or months. Their objective is simply to make a quick return on their investment.

The problem here is that the normally reliable market cannot assure the "efficiency" of transactions once power is separated from accountability. The lighting-fast in-and-out dealings of modern financiers assures two things: those who initiate the deals will not be around if things go sour and, as history records, power left unchallenged leads to excesses that eventually have to be corrected.

As an indicator of the rise in institutional influence in the stock exchanges, table 2.3 shows the significant increases in average daily volume and turnover of shares on the New York Stock Exchange from 1960 to 1985 – of which a majority is attributable to large trades of 10,000 share blocks. The sharp acceleration in turnover of such large trades, in particular, bears the unmistakable stamp of the institutional investor. Moreover, since some portion of institutional trading is in less than 10,000 share lots, the figures in table 2.3 considerably understate the degree of influence of institutions on trading.

Another dramatic change that influenced the relationship between firms and investors was the evolution of the role of the capital market itself. An unheralded cycle of growth and expansion of business in the late nineteenth and early twentieth centuries prompted the creation of new and more creative means of finance. Firms no longer could rely solely on the reinvestment of earnings plus capital supplied by bankers, business partners, or small and informal sources of funds. As demand for capital

Table 2.3 New York Stock Exchange trading

Year	Average daily share volume (millions of shares)	Turnover rate (%)	Large trades of 10,000 shares (% of total volume)
1960	3.0	12	na
1965	6.2	14	3
1970	11.6	19	15
1975	18.6	21	17
1980	44.9	36	29
1985	109.2	54	52

Source: *New York Stock Exchange Fact Book*, 1986, pp. 69–71.

mushroomed, especially permanent equity capital for investment in growing businesses, organized stock exchanges like the New York Stock Exchange emerged to fill the void. As conceived, the capital market was
intended to promote competition between the supply of, and demand for,
funds. As in any free market, it was to serve as a vehicle for allocating
resources among many buyers and sellers so as to achieve an equilibrium
among the various interests. In a democratic society, such market activity
is deemed essential for fair and impartial decisions in all facets of everyday
life, from selling produce, to selling products, to selling securities.

In the beginning, the market was an open system characterized by
interaction between many individual investors and large numbers of small
firms that represented the market's famed "invisible hand." By affording a
marketplace where opposing interests could compete fairly, the capital
market exerted a discipline that assured, as an end result, an efficient
allocation of scarce financial resources to their most fruitful employment.
But as firms matured, the frequency and urgency for capital infusions from
the capital market declined. The build-up of internal cash flows could
increasingly satisfy a greater part of firms' investment demands. Naturally,
managers turned first to this captive source of cash. This did not induce
managements to fritter capital away recklessly. To do so would jeopardize
the very survival of the firm and endanger the livelihoods of top management. What it did instead was force the markets to adjust.

Although the capital market still exerts a discipline, it is now felt mainly
by traders in outstanding securities rather than by corporate treasurers. A
high level of trading volume on the New York Stock Exchange and other
stock exchanges reveals a continued use of the capital market. A small
fraction of this trading represents new equity issues by big business as well
as modest amounts of new capital for small firms going public. In the main,
however, the market is no longer a reservoir for equity capital that firms
regularly draw from in order to fuel growth and expansion. Its key function
at present is to supply the liquidity that supports a deep and broad market
for trading and speculation in already issued securities.

In every important respect, the reality of a world in which owners
controlled firms by virtue of active participation as managers is permanently shattered. The market's decline as a provider of equity diminishes
its traditional role as the engine of corporate growth, and its emergence as
a trading medium works to benefit securities investors rather than business
firms.

Concentrations of power in large corporations and large institutional
investors is a picture far removed from Adam Smith's imagination. Both
the supply and demand side of the capital market have evolved beyond
what the drafters of a competitive marketplace theory could foresee. In the
original formulation, the marketplace played the all-important role and

market participants were mere epiphenomenon. In order to keep the integrity of this concept, the capital market had to retain its key role. A new economic theory (the theory of agency – see the subsection so entitled) was developed in order to preserve the centrality of markets. From this view, bilateral transactions between firms and investors are mediated by the capital market. As agents for stockholders – a firm's legal owners – management's first duty is to maximize shareowners' profits and thereby indirectly also to assure the maximum efficiency of the firm. If managers are tempted to stray from their appointed taks, the ultimate discipline through the capital market of a takeover of the firm or the removal of management will dissuade them. Whether the newly constructed theory "fits" as more than a legal fiction is untested. What casual observation and management practices suggest, however, is an imperfect capital market capable of being influenced by immense concentrations of financial power in pursuit of self-interests that are not necessarily coincident with those of society or those of firms' other stakeholders.

Agency theory The so-called "theory of agency" postulates that agents (managers) should in principle be working for the betterment of the principals (shareholders), who are the firm's legal owners.[32] Since this happy coincidence might not occur if managers were free to pursue their own self-interest, the capital market is the medium for bringing both parties' interests into alignment, and the level of stock prices acts as the index for how well or poorly management is carrying out its assignment. When managers' actions are less than optimal, or inefficient, stock prices will decline, causing the creation of an investment opportunity for someone to seize control and return the firm to its "natural" level of profitability. Other transgressions by managers such as inflated salaries, abuse of office, or personal aggrandizement would also be automatically reflected in stock prices and adjusted by the self-correcting actions of the capital market.

The upshot of agency theory is to retain the capital market's central role in enforcing firm efficiency by allocating investment capital to its best use. Even if firms do not go to the capital market and investors are not small and numerous, the interaction of supply and demand works as perfectly as it ever did – in theory. As in economics generally, the support for economists' views of how things work depends on positive thinking. If one assumes stock prices always reflect true value, then prices can be used as proxies for firm efficiency. And if one further assumes that deviations from such values will be recognized by market participants and bring prompt remedial action, then nothing tangible has been lost by ignoring evolutionary changes of the last two hundred or so years.

Whereas in most markets, direct interaction between buyers and sellers is needed to assure efficient outcomes, capital market efficiency has to be imagined. Firms do not actually compete with investors as a rule so that the desired objective of firm efficiency is only hypothetically subject to the market's invisible hand. A number of things have to be taken at face value in order for this perception of linkages between firms–markets–investors to work. First, the market has to be efficient, in the sense that stock prices continuously reflect "true" value, and that prices cannot be unduly influenced by non-value-creating activities. That is, the market cannot be fooled. Whenever stock prices move, a direct and proportionate change in efficiency is implied. Certain management actions and resulting stock-price effects strain one to believe the credibility of this proposition. Companies can buy back their stock, for example, which favorably affects earnings per share and thus stock prices. Thus money that could have been invested in productive plant and equipment may be used instead for near-term price appreciation. Firms also may assume more debt in order to pay out special dividends to shareowners. During the height of takeover activity in the 1980s, both practices were sometimes forced on management by financial speculators with large stock positions who directly benefited by such actions.

The market, in other words, can conceivably be "controlled" by the actions of the investors who comprise it. Only if the interest of investors and firms completely mesh will market efficiency work to the advantage of both, and even then the protection of other stakeholders' interests is not guaranteed. Firm efficiency, the cornerstone of economic theory, is not directly connected to stock prices. Only by a theoretical splicing of shareowners' interest with those of the firm are firm efficiency and stock prices made to move in unison. The elemental point, therefore, is not whether the market is efficient in reflecting shareowners' wealth, but whether efficiency in the pricing of shareowners' holdings is a sufficient condition to keep the capital market system as it is.

Capitalistic institutions – of which the capital market is a prominent symbol – need the support of the people, their elected representatives, and other institutions. To attempt to justify the capital market in terms only of its service to a relatively few shareowners is patently offensive. Even if successful in the short term, broader economic, political, and moral issues must eventually prevail. A democracy cannot be run to serve the selfish interests of a particular group or to place one group's priorities over those of society as a whole. In a heated series of debates between Adolf Berle and Merrick Dodd of the Harvard Law School, Berle at first insisted that officers and directors held corporate powers in trust for shareowners. Later, however, upon reconsideration, Berle came down squarely in support of Dodd's argument for the greater good.[33]

In the final analysis, the basis for "shareholders' rights" rests on evanescent legal entitlements. On the issue of risk, shareowners' risk is only an economic one. In terms of power, none is in fact exerted over the firms that shareowners are technically said to control. There is absolutely no relationship between shareowners' actions as investors and the authority they are presumed to possess as owners. In perverse fashion, the real influence wielded by management is treated as fictional and the legal fiction of investors' powers as real. Together with a specific view of market "efficiency," shareowners' rights form the bulwark of the theoretical case for perfect competition. But this logic, although rigorous, is fictional and the abstraction works only if it is sheltered from the light of everyday experience.

Also, whereas the stock market is efficient in a mechanical sense, it is hardly infallible in its judgment of future value, nor unbiased in the way those value judgments are reached. The stock market cannot display more than the value judgments of those who make it up and it is subject to the influence of its most influential members. When groups of investors find a new method to gain unintended and unforeseen ways to affect market outcomes for personal advantage, the rules need changing. If the business of business is to remain business, restraint on Wall Street is necessary. And for this to be possible, market infallibility cannot be allowed as an impenetrable defense that guards the status quo, in disregard of changing times or towards whose ends the efficiency of the market works.

Efficiency is not necessarily good of and by itself. Is Willie Sutton, the famous bank robber, to be judged innocent of the crime of theft because he increased the "efficiency" with which money circulated? Jay Gould and Jesse Livermore, two notorious stock market speculators, provided liquidity to the stock market – and thereby improved its "efficiency" – every time they bought and sold stock, although many of their dealings would be illegal by today's standards. More pointedly, what inalienable "right" is possessed by someone who owns stock in a company for a day or a month or even a year to decide its fate? Society may ultimately decide that this is not a right worth preserving, a conclusion that can never be reached if markets are perceived as immaculately conceived.

Only in the United States is a financial goal of investing for stock market gains put before the business objective of investing in physical assets to improve firm efficiency. In most industrialized countries, the operating condition of the company is deemed to be of greater importance than the financial well-being of its nominal owners.

In Japan, management's aims are expressed in terms of business objectives, not financial objectives. Studies of Japanese managers, for example, found that they do not give high priority to maximization of shareowners' wealth.[34] A questionnaire survey comparing large public firms in the

United States and in Japan revealed a significant difference between the two groups: no Japanese firm said that increasing its share price was its most important objective, and only 0.2 percent (out of 894 firms) placed it as the second most important objective.[35] Part of this difference may be attributable to the distinctions between the groups of shareowners in the two countries. In Japan, most stock is held by stable shareowners, many of them banks who are also creditors and act as financial advisers to the companies in which they invest. The investment ties by banks are strong and long-lasting, reflecting a mutuality of interests similar to those of the owner–financier prototype in America's early history.

In the United States, the imagery of shareowners' rights forces every action of management to be seen from the perspective of shareowners' self-interests. In diversification strategy, for example, a common foreclosure to firms diversifying away from core businesses is that this is an option rightly reserved for shareowners. Shareowners can achieve diversification independently of firms by altering the portfolio mix of their investments.[36] From this premise, the conclusion is reached that firms should not diversify, unless they can do so in manner that shareowners cannot duplicate, such as creating synergy by combining like activities in a merger.[37]

Seeing investors through a one-way mirror prejudices every action of management in favor of investors, regardless of any other consideration. This is excusable only if the ownership and management are the same, as they were originally when owners were also managers. In modern times, however, it can force management to choose between actions designed primarily to benefit investors rather than to improve the firm. As previously noted, some companies have assumed heavy debt burdens in order to make special, one-time payouts to shareowners – usually in order to ward off a takeover attempt threatened by those same shareowners, as happened in the Holiday and Allegis Corporations, for example. As a consequence, a firm is left more vulnerable because funds that could have been invested in the company have been diverted to enrich a powerful stockholder group. If one sees the stockholders and the firm as a single entity, a mere transference of moneys from one pocket to another within the organization has taken place. If one views stockholders as a separate entity with separate interests, however, one party to the transaction has been diminished in order to reward the other. In tightly contested markets, the weakened financial condition of the firm leaves it more exposed to business cycles as well as unanticipated initiatives by its competitors.

The implication of raising shareowners' interests above all others is to neuter corporate managers. They are reduced to pawns in a game of monopoly played by shareowners with their common stocks. If falling demand or entrapment within decaying or declining industries threatens a firm's survival or a manager's livelihood, that is all right, because the shareowner can easily avoid any personal consequences by selling out. For the shareowner, there are always alternative investments to pursue. But management must go down with the ship. And the ship itself is deemed expendable.

Were managers to follow this strategic advice, they would be mere custodians. They would attend to details, but refrain from individual initiatives or leadership in order to anticipate change. If strictly obeyed, industry stability becomes the natural order of things. Companies born into food, or chemical, or electrical businesses would persevere in that line. Industries would stabilize and managements could pursue a predictable and programmable routine. The static equilibrium conditions in economics would become real. Unsurprisingly, these are not the chain of events that anyone with a passing familiarity with business could accept as realistic. What is especially puzzling, therefore, is the passivity of researchers in the strategic management field in accepting the far-fetched notion that those who do, invest, and those who cannot, manage. Not only does this turn management on its head, but it violates the basic principle of managerial choice, which underlies strategic management. Further, it robs strategic corporate-level planning of its most basic purpose: that is, to determine what business a firm should be in.

The fact that managers have tended to be oriented more to the firm than its shareowners does not imply that managers do not feel a responsibility to shareowners. Both managers and shareowners have vested stakes in a firm's profitability and success. What is new is temporary shareowners, who seek quick financial gain, put in a position to decide a firm's very existence. This places the "new" shareowner potentially in conflict with management. In the case of diversification strategy, for example, shareowners' freedom to diversify has not prevented firms from actively diversifying on their own. The long-term evolution of big business from a simple one-product focus to more diversified product lines and different lines of business is verified in Alfred Chandler's works and attested to repeatedly by the statements of top management.

Alfred Sloan, the pioneering leader of General Motors, recognized the futility of braking or slowing growth in big businesses. Progress and growth are intertwined, he reasoned, "for there is no resting place for an enterprise in a competitive economy."[38] Coincident with a firm's desire for growth is its emphasis on survival. Henry Singleton, the founder and chief executive of Teledyne, a major diversified firm constructed in the 1960s, expressed the managerial case for growth, diversification, and survival in plain language:

> The principal reason "to diversify" is the natural desire of companies to survive. If you remain in one single line, you will not survive.

Everything has its day. You can't wait to see what is going to replace what you are doing . . . Concurrent with the instinct for survival is the desire to grow . . . I'm talking about the long term.[39]

The difference in goals conveyed by management's statements as compared with the implication of shareowner's rights suggests a gap as yet unbridged. With over half a century of experience, the question of who "controls" is still unsettled. This issue is at the very essence of our capitalistic system. A resolution cannot be postponed for ever. Neither can a meaningful analysis start with a simplistic view that assumes perfect markets and considers only shareowners' rights. Rather, it requires an intensive investigation of our imperfect capital market system to see if it still adequately fulfills the expectations originally projected for it.

Myth 4: Specialization is the Key to Succesful Diversification

Efficiency of production is the economist's criterion for successful management, where efficiency is defined by specialization. Using cost as the index of efficiency, the division of work into minute details lowers costs by simplifying operations and thereby raising worker productivity. The more output for the same input serves the economist's dual goals of cost reduction and profit maximization. Raising this concept to the firm level, a company already successful in manufacturing one product is considered an especially good prospect for being successful by concentrating on investment that adds further capacity to build more of the same product. Extending this line of reasoning, the efficiency of production, and hence profits, will be maximized by staying with the business a firm knows best.

There is nothing wrong with this characterization, except that it is incomplete. Specialization is a desirable attribute at given times and under certain conditions, it is true. When technological advances in communications and transportation made mass production feasible in the United States – almost a century and a half ago – the emphasis was on adding capacity as markets opened up. Production was the problem, not demand. For some time, the emphasis rightly stayed on reinvesting profits back into productive capacity in order to make more of the same things. By combining specialization of labor with machine technology, costs declined and the efficiency of production was enhanced. With the opportunities afforded by new markets and expanding demand, the potential high return from reinvesting funds into making the same products eliminated any desire to diversify beyond a narrow specialization.

Eventually, however, markets reached saturation. The growth in demand tapered off and competition for shares in a more limited market became hotly contested. The natural life-cycle of products – from fast growth to maturity and eventual stability or decline – applied to individual firms as well. Facing slackening growth in revenues, companies naturally began to consider strategies for maintaining a satisfactory rate of expansion.

It is the exceptional large modern corporation that is still narrowly specialized. Over time, firms took the opportunity to diversify both internally and through acquisitions into a wide range of product lines and distinct new businesses. No giant corporation today is as specialized in its markets as when it began. As circumstances change, companies need to adapt in order to survive. Avoiding Schumpeter's "creative destruction" means growing beyond a core specialization. More specifically, companies become "creative" in order to avoid the entropy trap facing companies that cling to a static strategy.

Diversification, even into unrelated fields, does not invalidate or contradict the advantages of specialization. To the contrary, a firm that loses sight of the need to be efficient *in every business it is in* will invariably lose a competitive edge in overall efficiency and profitability. The goal of a multi-business firm is to manage effectively the scope of its total mix of operations, while keeping close tabs on the progress each individual unit is making. Justification of economies of scale (specialization) need not conflict with economies of diversification (scope). The two concepts are not competing or mutually exclusive – they are merely different. There is no inherent reason for firms to neglect economies of scale within business units merely because the scope of the corporation broadens. Many diversified companies obviously had to subscribe to a strategy of greater scope in order to attain their current breadth and mix of businesses.

Why is it that the motive for companies to diversify into new businesses escapes those who spend a career explaining firm behavior? One part of the explanation, perhaps, is overemphasizing the advantages of specialization, while overlooking those of diversification. In *In Search of Excellence*, Peters and Waterman rely entirely on the notion of specialization in order to justify a conclusion that companies should "stick to their knitting."[40] While listing a set of factors that would make companies more efficient, Peters and Waterman ignore the possibility that expertise can be applied to more than one business. Michael Porter, who wrote best sellers addressing both corporate- and business-level strategy, allows for some diversification, but *only* if expertise or other resources of the diversifying firm are transferable as the basis for the strategy.

A company's "value chain" – a central concept in Porter's analysis – defines a set of "primary" and "support" activities common to every company. It is a company's ability to use one or more of the activities in the value chain that permits successful branching out into other fields. Transferring "activity" skills or sharing activities are the bases for creating value that underlie Porter's view of diversification strategy.

Porter does not directly argue against firms diversifying into completely new businesses – through unrelated acquisitions primarily – but instead he defines unrelated as having "no clear opportunity to transfer skills or share important activities."[41] Since the primary and support activities that make up Porter's value chain are generic to *all* companies, every diversification holds the potential for at least a minimum of sharing of skills or activities. Only in the rare case of the pure holding company – where acquired businesses are not managed, but are held merely as investments – is there no operational contact between acquirer and acquiree. In every other case, there is some measure of commonality. Thus, every diversification could conceivably be viewed as "related," by Porter's measure. If acquisition of an entirely unfamiliar business succeeds, it could always be deemed to have benefited from skill transference or activity-sharing, and thus qualify as a related acquisition. If acquisition into an unfamiliar line of business fails, on the other hand, its failure can be blamed on its unrelatedness. Without defining a specific level of activity-sharing that defines relatedness, Porter has guaranteed the infallibility of his definition. Like a Delphic oracle, he can claim to have given the "right" answer whatever the outcome.

A practical example illustrates the conundrum in Porter's method. When Dr Pepper, the soft-drink maker, entered the bottling business, management thought it was making a related diversification. After a disastrous earnings experience, it was apparent that bottling just *appeared* to be related; it did not fit with Dr Pepper's soft-drink business at all. The moral seems to be "if it works, it's a core business."[42]

Procter & Gamble is another company where relatedness is a concept without clear meaning, if Porter's definition is relied upon. For example, Procter & Gamble is cited by Porter as a company successful in becoming the leader in children's Pampers (disposable diapers) because it "employs a common distribution system and sales force in both paper towels and disposable diapers."[43] Yet Porter ignores the other parts of the value chain in the manufacture and sale of diapers that are fundamentally different from Procter & Gamble's expertise in soaps and detergents.

Procter & Gamble has also diversified into pharmaceuticals, this time through acquisitions. Three major acquisitions – Norwich-Eaton, Richardson-Vicks, and Monsanto's G.D. Searle unit – place it in the new area of over-the-counter drugs. In any normal sense, these acquisitions are unrelated to Procter & Gamble's basic soap and detergents business. Although Procter & Gamble will logically try to use its marketing expertise and distribution muscle as levers for competitive advantage, the dissimilarities of this new venture contrast in many ways from Procter & Gamble's core specialization. Does the employment by Procter & Gamble of *any* part of its value chain in managing an acquisition justify an otherwise unrelated acquisition? By this standard, a move by Procter & Gamble into the fast-food business, or the sale of wines and spirits, or automobile dealerships, or any business dealing with direct marketing to retail customers could be stretched to "fit" with Procter & Gamble's competence.

Ambiguity in Porter's analysis is compounded when Porter states elsewhere that doing "something for shareholders that they can do themselves is not a basis for corporate strategy."[44] As it is traditionally interpreted, and as Porter seems to agree, shareholders' ability to readily diversify their own portfolio of stocks precludes the need for companies to diversify for them. Yet Porter goes on to argue that if diversification "adds value," it is a proper strategy. Which advice is management to follow? Value *ex ante* is a judgment call. No company deliberately pursues a flawed strategy. There are frequent occasions, however, where value is perceived, but no real advantage subsequently materializes. Without objective guidelines to distinguish related from unrelated, or what creates value from what does not, management is on its own in evaluating the appropriateness of undertaking a specific acquisition.

Relying on either the Federal Trade Commission's definition of acquisitions as unrelated when they are neither horizontal nor vertical in nature, or the Standard Industrial Classification system for defining industry boundaries, the majority of big firms are widely diversified. Most of these companies began by a portfolio strategy of diversification, and only later integrated acquisitions as passage of time and experience allowed for a successful transition. Here again, Porter seems disingenuous, disapproving generally of portfolio-style diversification "unless [firms] can integrate the acquisition."[45] This amounts to approval of all portfolio-style acquisitions that work.

Alfred Chandler has provided clear-cut evidence that firms unable to integrate acquisitions tend to fail or underperform. After a major acquisition, companies that are ultimately successful will move to build an overall corporate system that binds all the various business units into a coherent organization. Those companies that do not do this become the failures and also-rans of the nation's big businesses. Portfolio-style diversification is often necessary in order to begin the process of diversifying away from core businesses. Integration *follows*, but cannot be used to prejudge the merits of a particular acquisition.

Also, integration is a matter of degree. Diversified companies cannot be as tightly integrated as single-product companies without losing the advantages they sought to achieve through diversification. Only by operating in distinct and separate businesses can economies of scope be maximized. And in that situation, the organizational structure must change in order to accommodate the strategy, with greater autonomy for each business and less hierarchical controls from the top. Conversely, a one-product firm is the quintessential case for economies of specialization. To say a diversified company should be integrated, therefore, says little more than that it should operate somewhere between the polar extremes of total autonomy in a holding-company type of structure and total integration in a one-product firm.

At its core, Porter's strategy of diversification for the firm amounts to an extension of the concept of specialization in each individual business unit. By basing his views on industrial organization economics, Porter starts with a model that assumes corporations compete within stable industry structures. Porter modifies the strict assumptions of industrial organization to allow for managerial initiatives and differences of skill and technology among firms. Another modification is to allow acquisition entry as well as internal diversification. Porter, however, chose to retain an assumption of *relatively* stable industry boundaries. If industries could freely be breached, industrial organization's primary thesis, and the basis for Porter's own analysis, would be seriously compromised. Basically, Porter tries to straddle two positions. He keeps one foot in economics' world of stability and market-driven competition, while relaxing the strictness of these conditions in order to take account of managerial initiatives and strategy-making. In the end, the effort only partially succeeds. Firm individuality and an emphasis on survival and growth are inimical to industrial organization's concepts. Diversification for economies of scope at the corporate level is not even part of either mainstream economics or industrial organization economics. *There is no need for a corporate level in economics' model of one-product firms.*

In adapting industrial organization's views for his strategy of diversification, Porter was biased from the beginning to a business-level orientation. Porter's optimum diversification foresees an acquired company that utilizes all parts of the parent company's value chain. This would assure the maximum in skill transference and resource-sharing. The epitome would be a horizontal acquisition: a company buying out an industry competitor, for example, Ford buying Chrysler. On the other hand, this would defeat the purpose for companies diversifying in the first place: to avoid the limitations of industries that require specialized skills or assets no longer in demand. United States Steel's strategy of diversifying into the energy business, for example, was a direct result of the limited growth perceived in steel and related industries. Attempting to diversify into businesses close to steel would only have committed United States Steel even more to an industry seen to be in a long-term decline. The option in this and similar cases is *to take a calculated risk* by diversifying into an unrelated business.

Also, Porter's articulated case for diversification does not reflect managers' motives. Except for clear cases of horizontal or vertical acquisitions, companies have not singled out specialization or integration as strategic priorities in choosing new businesses to enter. Overall, few, if any corporations have taken as calculated and circumscribed a view to acquisitions as Porter suggests is desirable. Conagra, for example, is a diversified food company that made a number of acquisitions, but not in the businesses it would have predicted or chosen. None of the acquisitions in frozen foods, flour milling, or meat products neatly fit Conagra's expressed plans to move into commodity-type businesses like poultry. Based on its experience, the company modified its ideal criteria into a pragmatic approach to expansion: for example, any food-related company with significant market shares, good management, and low product costs is a potential acquisition target. None of these criteria mesh with a strategy based solely on specialization, either as traditionally conceived, or as Porter's value-chain analysis would suggest. Yet this defensible alternative basis for diversification is one that has served Conagra extremely well.

Ryder System is another case where diversification worked, even though the company moved into apparently diverse lines of business. In 1974, on the verge of bankruptcy, Ryder hired a new chief executive officer and began an active acquisition program, making over sixty acquisitions within four years. The company established itself in such diverse lines as full service leasing, aviation repair and parts distribution, general freight trucking, and management of school bus fleets, among others. Ryder ranged far afield in order to pick situations where management is friendly, and the company fits somewhere in the services industry. There undoubtedly are skills that transfer among some of the acquisitions Ryder made, but just as clearly the overall strategy cannot be explained on that basis alone, since the mix of businesses often bears little affinity with the core specialization of renting trucks. Because Ryder moved so quickly, and acquired so many diverse operations, it ran the risk of losing control of the enterprise it built. On the other hand, without taking risks, a company in a mature industry can doom itself to an even more precarious and predictable dead-end.

At issue, fundamentally, is whether skills are hereditary or whether they can be acquired. Is a company sealed for ever in the industry it was born into and limited by the skills endemic to that industry? The answer revolves around a static or dynamic view of history. Schumpeter made change an endemic aspect of progress. According to mainstream economics, however, the market view of economic progress denies firms and their managers a useful decision-making role. Managerial learning and adaptation is a futile expectation, since, according to economics, it is the market that determines outcomes, regardless of what institutions and individuals do. This fatalistic view impressed Chandler as an odd position for economists to have taken in light of all the evidence of proactive administrative changes and adaptations that have characterized the growth of big business in the United States.

Before deciding on an appropriate industrial policy, the United States should study the Japanese experience. In 1950, with the United States' automobile market securely in the grasp of domestic firms, no preparations were made to counter the successful invasion of this industry by Japanese competitors. Indeed, the economist's law of specialization gave no reason for domestic car producers to be concerned. Japanese success could be better assured by staying with labor-intensive industries like textiles, where Japan enjoyed a distinct comparative advantage. Instead, Japan took a seemingly no-win strategy of deliberately targeting progressive moves into industries where rapid growth and high demand were foreseen, but where Japan was lacking in expertise. Japan's logic proved far-sighted, as it turned out, but hardly fortuitous, as the following account by a Japanese official relates:

> The Ministry of International Trade and Industry decided to establish in Japan industries which require intensive employment of capital and technology, industries that in consideration of comparative cost of production should be the most inappropriate for Japan, industries such as steel, oil refining, petro-chemicals, automobiles, aircraft, industrial machinery of all sorts, and later electronics, including electronic computers. From a short-run, static viewpoint, encouragement of such industries would seem to conflict with economic rationalism. But, from a long-range point of view, these are precisely the industries where income elasticity of demand is high.[46]

There is always a temptation to get comfortable doing what a firm knows best. This works optimally, however, in settings where industries, competitors, and environments are relatively stable. With the introduction of new technologies or better strategies by competitors, firms that remain rooted in tradition are vulnerable. Expansion within a single industry is eventually reined by a slowing in market growth and technological innovation. When these twin driving forces decline, but competition is strong or increases, profitability and even the survival of the firm are imperiled. Much of the emphasis for diversification in today's companies was in order to escape the confines of "old" industries. Where diversification succeeded, as it has in many firms, it had to overcome the lack of specialization's advantage. The concept of specialization allows no progression over time beyond a seminal idea for building a product or delivering a service. Like a perverse distortion of Darwinism, the more advanced species in the business population gain nothing from their accumulated knowledge and experience. The repositioning of a company away from its industry is outside any economic theory's range of admissible evolution. The motivations and justification behind diversification into new industries scarcely receive serious notice. By comparison, a veritable library of books has been written by economists and management academics on the reasons why such diversification is doomed to failure. It is time, in the light of the evidence, to redress this imbalance by admitting the "pros" of unrelated diversification as well as the "cons" against specialization.

Myth 5: Diversity cannot be Managed

If all else fails, the inability to manage is a fall-back position against complex diversification. This tactical defense was first used against large size. As companies got bigger, the diminishing ability to control far-flung units was said to limit expansion. At some point, the economies of scale would be offset by the diseconomies of complex management. As companies continued to expand, the upper boundaries of size kept escalating. At present, the assertion that there are absolute limits to size is no longer a respectable contention. The presumed limit on size has collapsed under the sheer weight of evidence pressing against it. A corollary scenario, it seems, is being played out in the case of complex diversification: that is, diversification through acquisitions that remove a company from its core business cannot be managed. The more new businesses that companies try to digest, the more likely they are to suffer corporate indigestion, so to speak.

As in the case of specialization, there is some truth to the charges. A random spread into many businesses, rapidly assembled and loosely controlled, undoubtedly heightens the risk of a management meltdown. As long as a core business constitutes a dominant share of the total, it provides a stable base for corporate diversification. This stability becomes weaker as companies move into more product-markets distant from their organizational center. By going further afield, the necessity for creating a structure and strategy for administrative control becomes increasingly pressing.

Conglomerates formed between the mid-1950s and mid-1960s were frequently portrayed as examples of impending organizational disasters. The Federal Trade Commission's analogy of a far-fetched merger between "a ship builder and an ice-cream manufacturer" conveyed general skepticism of conglomerate strategy. In fact, some conglomerates seemed to be trying to live up to critics' worst expectations. ITT – once known as the biggest conglomerate on earth – at one time or other had acquired its way into such businesses as forest products, hotels, food and bakery products, machinery, insurance, finance, energy, electronics, and a hodgepodge of smallish miscellaneous units. Gulf and Western (G + W), another of the earliest and most aggressive conglomerates, moved rapidly to assemble a corporate smorgasbord consisting of cement, zinc, paper, sugar, hosiery, refrigeration equipment, movies, finance, publishing, mattresses, and on and on. There is little apparent motive other than managerial indulgence to justify such a *melange* of acquisitions. No sane person would seriously propose this style of diversification as a corporate model for others to follow, and certainly not as a prescription that would serve the national and international interests of the country.

The impression of the eternally acquisitive conglomerate has become a convenient stereotype for deriding unrelated acquisitions in general. The failings of some conglomerate empires provided "proof" for those persons already convinced that unrelated diversification made no sense. However, a wholesale indictment of unrelated diversification will not stand scrutiny. Many former conglomerates have become more focused, casting off the acquisitions that added bulk, but did not do much for profits. Slimming down not only raised the overall profitability of the enterprise, but also reduced the problem of administrative management. Instead of a giant made of dwarfs, successful diversified companies assembled a few heavy-weight groups.

Now, it is popular to perceive reformed conglomerates – most of which have interests in several major unrelated fields – as having "focused mass." G + W is a good case in point. Charles Bluhdorn, the conglomerate's founder and chief acquisitor, hardly met a company he did not want to buy. By the time Martin Davis took over, after Bluhdorn's untimely death, G + W had dozens of different product lines. Following a period of divestment and consolidation, Davis developed what business writers now admiringly promote as an example of superior diversification. The conglomerate frog has become a prince. None the less, G + W is still a varied multi-business corporation. The three current areas of concentration – entertainment, publishing, and financial services – provide wide umbrellas under which a considerable number of individual and distinct business units are sheltered.

What G + W did was to make the logical, and necessary, trade-off between control and diversification. Maximizing control by specializing, versus maximizing risk/reward by diversifying, are the extremes in a spectrum of managerial choices. For big companies with large positions in mature industries, neither of these options is likely to represent an ideal.

The uneven success in managing diversity in the past can only be partially blamed on complexity. More accurately, it reflects bad strategy in diversifying before management has a good plan in mind, and lack of management skills in administering the businesses once they had been acquired. Given a sound strategy, sufficient time, and managerial competence, there is no demonstrable limit to the level of diversity a company might achieve and profitably control. Just as giant integrated corporations overcame the management obstacles to large size, diversified companies can overcome the limitations of complexity. Whether companies grow large or more complex, the major restraint is managerial. Yet, until Alfred Chandler's writings related administrative structure with strategy, administrative management was given no role in explaining the adaptation of corporations to successive periods of transition and metamorphosis. By omitting consideration of the main mechanism for change, the tendency was to disbelieve that radical change could occur.

Unfortunately, analysis of the potential of diversification still suffers from the identification of multi-business companies with a limiting form of organizational structure: the holding company. Unlike centrally administered operating companies, pure holding companies exercise no control over individual units. Until companies establish a managerial hierarchy, holding companies, as commonly thought of, represent little more than a federation of autonomous specialized subsidiaries.[47]

Holding companies were especially popular among public utilities in the United States prior to the great stock market crash in 1929. Overextended financial structures were typical in the utility industry. From 1929 to 1936, over fifty holding companies with combined securities having a par value of $1.7 billion went into receivership or bankruptcy. Losses by shareholders were catastrophic. Remembered ingloriously for the magnitude of his excess was Samuel Insull, who had put together the Middle West Utilities Company only to watch its price decline from a high of $57 a share in 1929 to less than a dollar in 1932.[48]

Persistence in using a holding-company structure in managing many independent business units risks pulling the entire enterprise down due to economic misfortune in one or more of the uncontrolled subsidiaries. The ability to progress from a loose operating structure to an integrated administrative system has been a distinguishing mark of successful diversified corporations in the past. A transition from relative autonomy to integration has occurred in major European countries as well, according to the account by Alfred Chandler and Herman Daems:

> In Germany, businessmen more often made use of the cartel; in Britain, the industry-wide holding company; and in France, the industrial group tied together by financial holdings. By the 1970s however, the centrally controlled, incorporated operating enterprise [in the United States] had become the normal instrument for carrying on big business in all four economies.[49]

In spite of the historical record, only relatively recently has the formal literature on diversification conceded the possibility that companies might successfully traverse from passive holding companies to administered operating companies.[50]

Mysteriously, there is little justification or explanation of how the holding-company species came into being in the first place. In equilibrium statics, evolution just happens. Different organizational structures at separate times are accepted without regard to how they came to be. Unrelated diversification, for example, is disparaged, while simultaneously addressing how best to manage diversity. This preoccupation with symptoms, but

not with causes is a curious intellectual trait. To disregard how auton-
omously run subsidiaries become integrated into an administered and
diversified corporation is to miss the phenomenon most worthy of study.

Of all aspects of diversification, the most inadequately treated is administration. Since Alfred Chandler wrote on multidivisional structures, a
form already commonly in use by the 1930s, virtually no further conceptual
insights combining advances in structures with changes in strategy have
emerged. Having neglected the administrative side of diversification for so
long, there is an awkwardness in coming to grips with this dimension now.
Oliver Williamson, an exceptional economist who has something good to
say about diversification, classifies and discusses Chandler's organizational
concepts as three symbolic types: M, H, and U. He views the M form
(multidivisional structure) as the preferred way for diversified companies
to organize and the natural successor design to U forms (functional
structures) used by firms concentrated around a single core business. There
is little merit seen in H forms (holding companies), merely mentioned,
apparently, to illustrate an organizational trap waiting for the unsuspecting
diversifier.

But if H-form structures have so little to recommend them, why do they
exist at all? Williamson does not adequately address this point.[51] Attributable perhaps to his training in static equilibrium analysis, Williamson fails
to perceive the need for transitional structures in going from a tightly
organized company concentrated in a single business, or closely related
businesses, into a full-fledged multi-business corporation. Getting from
one stage of growth to the other involves time in transition and an
organizational bridge from one structure to another. Because a long
learning process is unavoidable in managing innovative changes in
strategy, administrative competence may lag strategic change by years, if
not decades.

Moreover, there is not a single M type of design for diversified companies,
as Williamson implies. Instead, there are several variations in order
to accord with the different strategic approaches to diversification. Because
of the lag between creation of a new strategy and evolution of an appropriate administrative system, a discernible pattern of matching strategies and
structures is not yet obvious. Figure 2.1B, however, suggests two points of
differentiation that are basic: "passive" holding companies versus "operational" multi-business structures.

Under a passive holding-company arrangement, the investor–owner has
no intention of taking an active management role. The "holding" company
treats its investments with a detachment reminiscent of an average stockholder. The second category puts forth three administrative structures
where top management is involved, in varying degrees, in actively managing a number of businesses. (Strategies associated with each of the three

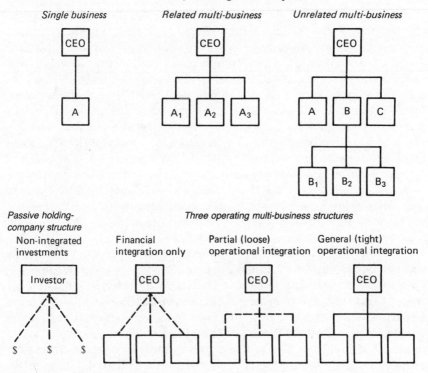

CEO Chief executive officer.

Figure 2.1 A Three static organizational structures
B Passive holding company versus three transitional operating structures

structures shown in figure 2.1 are discussed in chapter 4.) The degree of top management involvement is progressive. In a financial style of management, for example, administrative coordination is secondary. Primary interest is in using finance as a tool for building a business empire rather than managing it. The next system intensifies top management's coordination and control, although each business still enjoys a high degree of autonomy. Here, businesses might be strategically grouped to reflect a common strategy – with different companies operating within a single broad theme: for example, "consumer goods," "industrial products," "financial services," "defense," etc. – as opposed to an emphasis on random accumulation, a trait characteristic of purely financially-oriented diversification. Sharing a common orientation reduces complexity of managing totally unfamiliar businesses. It also allows parent companies to use expertise, on a limited scale, to develop synergy with their acquisitions. The final "general-integration" structure in figure 2.1 suggests the strongest organizational glue cementing the various parts of the corporation together. Here, sharing of intangibles like a common culture, organizational goals, and company image unify what appear on the surface as dissimilar businesses run with a large degree of autonomy.

Failing to distinguish between "passive" and "active" multi-business organizations creates confusion when reading the literature on business development as well as when attempting to apply principles of organizational design in practice. RJR–Nabisco, for example, with more than two full generational cycles of diversification behind it, had described itself publicly as using a "holding-company" style of management. Clearly, RJR–Nabisco's management did not desire to mold itself into a passive holding company. References to a holding-company preference by RJR–Nabisco and other firms generally mean movement toward greater degrees of autonomy-afforded business units by the parent corporation, depending on what strategic evaluation suggests is desirable.

In RJR–Nabisco's case, imagined synergies to bind one food business to another were found to be non-existent. Despite numerous corporate reorganizations and management reshufflings, RJR–Nabisco finally concluded that the hoped-for synergies between Nabisco's cookie and cracker business and Del Monte's fresh fruit and canned vegetable business simply did not exist. Del Monte "marches to an entirely different tempo," said a top Del Monte official, and to try and force integration would cause each business to miss opportunities and fall short of its potential.[52] Thus RJR–Nabisco formed itself into three separate operating businesses: Reynolds Tobacco, Del Monte, and Nabisco, each with its own chief executive officer (prior to the company being purchased by Kohlberg Kravis Roberts). In effect, the parent chose to manage an "operating multi-business," while reorganizing in order to provide greater distance between two of its major units. Implicitly, RJR–Nabisco elected something between the extremes of simple "financial integration" and "general integration" as its management style. (Since writing this, however, RJR–Nabisco has become a private company through a leveraged buyout, with restructuring implications that would have a greater impact on its organizational structure.)

Transition from a closely-knit single business to a closely-knit complex of different businesses infers a long interim period of adjustment, during which tight administrative coordination and control must slacken. At one extreme, General Electric is a typical example of a tightly-integrated multi-business. A cohesiveness among General Electric's top managers exists. In 1986, Jack Welch, the chief executive officer, created the Corporate Executive Council to bring together the fourteen leaders of each major business, heads of the corporate staff departments, and Welch's top corporate-level management team. The sharing that results is designed to build a stronger organization focused on common goals and objectives, even though each business is run almost as a separate company. In essence, the operating units are decentralized at the business level in order to assure flexibility in responding to competitive opportunities and threats, while centralized sharing of values across businesses assures that each business is a team player.

Over time, General Electric has painstakingly adapted its organizational structure to match its strategy and is constantly fine-tuning the process. Newly diversified companies, on the other hand, venturing into new businesses for the first time, or assembling a number of different businesses over a short span of time, face formidable administrative hurdles before approximating General Electric's degree of administrative competence. How much unrelatedness there is to manage, and in what space of time, has a great impact on the adjustment problem. Different cultures, old-manager networks, and normal infighting for status and capital will extend the period of adjustment. In such cases, a loosely-integrated structure with regard to new businesses makes sense as an interim phase.

In comparison to a cooperative "family of businesses," newly-formed multi-business corporations can at first resemble "warring tribes." Until systems and controls for integrating operations can be implemented, the new and old parts of a company cannot operate successfully in unison. To date, very little attention has been given on how to manage in order to bridge periods of change and adjustment. Duplicating the statics of economics, the management profession has devoted a considerable effort to counseling companies on how to manage within an assumed state of affairs, but comparatively little on the necessary structural adaptations that accompany changes in strategy. In particular, complex multi-business organizations have been virtually overlooked.

Ready examples of good and bad management exist in specialized and diversified companies alike. A number of companies made strategic *faux pas* by staying in industries like leather, coal, and steel. Major realignments within industries have also toppled once-dominant companies (Bank of America and International Harvester spring to mind). Management history reminds us that it is complacency rather than size or complexity that presents the ultimate danger for companies. For all the criticism directed at unrelated diversification, for instance, research shows that of the twenty-five companies on the *Fortune 500* list that gave the highest returns to shareholders from 1970–87, fifteen were in multiple businesses.[53] In the end, management determines industry performance, not the reverse.

Myth 6: Global and Domestic Competition Present the Same Problems

One of the most difficult decisions a corporate manager encounters is taking action in *anticipation* of change. The penalty for being wrong can be severe professionally, while the chances of successful innovation are problematic. This creates a bias, especially in large public corporations, for *measured* innovation.

For many years, American industry had little to fear from foreign competition. Contests for market shares tended to settle into a vigorous, but predictable set of tactics, with domestic competitors' moves only marginally different from one another. The result was a build-up of inertia. When Japanese companies introduced new means for gaining competitive advantage, there was no quick retaliation by United States firms. Only later, when it was too late for many companies and industries, did radical changes ensue. Even now, many companies are trying to catch up. Teams of experts travel to Japan in a reversal of the old student–teacher relationship, with the United States managers trying to adapt Japanese methods in order to improve their level of competitiveness with the Japanese.

Another watershed in international competition may be around the corner, although, once again, the conventional wisdom may not apply. Even while multinational companies aggressively acquire and merge in order to build up global positions within industries, a restructuring across industries looms on the horizon. Japan and Korea, the two leading industrialized nations in the Pacific, possess the wherewithal to demonstrate the advantages of complex diversification that the United States is reluctant to grasp or seriously investigate. If size plus diversity yield competitive advantage, it is knowledge that will have been acquired at great expense, if a first-mover advantage is conceded.

Taking Japanese and Korean corporations as examples, there are several reasons why they could become even more formidable adversaries in any future inter-industry competition. First, they are already masters in managing multi-business diversification. Based on family-style management, large corporations that resemble conglomerates – called *keiretsu* in Japan and *chaebol* in Korea – have evolved primarily by branching out internally into fast-growth markets by utilizing the skills or resources of the parent. They come close to meeting Michael Porter's diversification criteria based on skill transference or resource-sharing. In fact, Porter's analysis applies much better to internal rather than external diversification, and in the particular style of Japanese and Korean management instead of US practices.

For example, Yamaha, a leading Japanese conglomerate, capitalized on metallurgy skills developed in the production of motorcycles by applying them to the manufacturing of musical instruments. Yamaha's machine technology in motorcycles also found application in the manufacture of snowmobiles, outboard motors, golf carts, and jet skis. In addition, Yamaha produces compact-disk players and furniture. Samsung, the largest of Korea's conglomerates with revenues of $24 billion in 1987, has major operations in consumer electronics, semi-conductors, sugar, and paper. Of Korea's ten largest conglomerates, a spread into at least three major and distinct industries is typical. These conglomerate superpowers have developed organizations of "managed diversity" that provide a springboard for expanding into new businesses. Acquisition of foreign companies, including American firms, could be assimilated into one of the existing "family businesses" or integrated as a new member in the "corporate family." Either way, mastery of the art of managing conglomerates could give an enormous edge that most United States firms still lack.

However, the cohesion from family-style management found in Japan and Korea cannot be copied in the United States, mainly for cultural and legal reasons. In Japan, there is an interlocking arrangement among large stockholder groups, including banks, suppliers, and institutional investors, all of which are loyal to the corporation. Further, reciprocal ownership of shares among companies in the same group of related firms is common. This "corporate collectivism" fosters a strong mutuality of interest among Japanese combinations like Mitsubishi, Mitsui, and Sumitomo, to name just three. Japan's Yamaha is actually two separate and public companies headed by a single chairman. Although the chairman owns a relatively small percentage of either firm, there is little question that he is in control. According to Japanese custom, a company is considered to be held in trust by the founder to be passed on to his heirs and they to future generations. Selling a company in order to make a profit is not a popular notion, with corporate takeovers tagged with the same word used to describe hijacking: *nottori*.

A third reason why these collective giants can operate more efficiently than US multi-business firms is an enduring dedication to a strategy of progressive diversification. Taking the lead from their governments, corporations in Japan and Korea feel a need to deploy capital intensively into emerging industries and away from declining industries. In carrying out this philosophy, Japanese and Korean companies are continually in transition. The new head of Samsung displays the same sense of urgency that characterized his father, the former chief executive officer, and previous family corporate leaders: "If we don't move into more capital- and technology-intensive industries, our very survival may be at stake."[54] In developing its industrial strategy, Samsung copied the pattern set down by Japan in moving stage-by-stage through increasingly advanced levels of industrial complexity.

In the 1950s Lee [Samsung's CEO] prospered by dominating cash generating consumer necessities like sugar, wool, textiles and flour in an impoverished nation. In the 1960s he entered paper, electronics, fertilizers, retailing and life insurance. In the 1970s and early 1980s, Lee drove ahead first into petrochemicals, hotels and construction, and then into semiconductors, computers, aerospace, genetic engineering and robots. Note that Samsung is much less concentrated in heavy industry than Hyundai or Daewoo [two other leading conglomerates].[55]

Fouth, United States firms are effectively blocked from having the equal access to acquisitions in Japan that Japanese firms have in the United States. Acquisitions by foreigners, especially unfriendly ones, of Japanese and Korean firms are the exception. Cross-holdings of stock among firms keep most of the shares out of circulation. Extreme loyalty to domestic firms precludes unfriendly takeovers, and friendly mergers and acquisitions are possible only after many years of building inter-firm confidence and trust. With the most open market for stock transactions, the United States places itself at a bilateral disadvantage, should either Japan or Korea initiate an active program of diversifying into US industries through acquisitions. In particular, if Japanese or Korean conglomerates were to decide that acquisitions were the preferred route to foreign markets, their wide network of businesses could mark just about any industry group for entry, and their financial resources would make all but the largest US companies potential targets.

Prospects for a future trend toward global competition among big businesses on an inter-industry scale has historical and economic precedents. Since the mid-nineteenth century, a five-stage evolution of big business in the United States has been defined. Foreign trading partners with the United States are currently imitating the penultimate phase of that pattern.

In the first stage, American companies grew big to achieve economies of large scale. At phase two, horizontal and vertical diversification allowed companies to consolidate market power and control key supply and distribution functions. Stage three involved international diversification. In the fourth stage, companies diversified into related businesses by emphasizing research and development, adding new products, and then increasingly through mergers and acquisitions. The final stage is inter-industry diversification using acquisitions.

Advanced multinational companies are actively engaged in the fourth stage: enlarging market positions in foreign markets by way of horizontal acquisitions. A global overcapacity in key industries like the motor industry, heavy equipment, textiles, and even computers, is compelling reason for firms to rationalize international operations and markets. A number of

Table 2.4 Large US acquisitions by foreign companies

Acquirer (nationality)	Acquiree	Industry of acquiree
Aoki (Japan), with Bass Group (USA)	Westin, a part of Allegis Corporation	hotels and resorts
Bat industries (UK)	Farmers Group	insurance
Beazer PLC (UK)	Koppers	diversified chemicals
Bertelsmann (German)	Doubleday	book publisher
Bridgestone (Japan)	Firestone	rubber tires
British Petroleum (UK)	Standard Oil (Ohio)	oil and gas
Broken Hill Proprietary Australian)	Utah International	natural resources
Campeau (Canadian)	Allied Stores and ˙Federated	department stores
Compagnie Générale d' Electricité (French)	Telecom, part of ITT	telecommunications
Dainippon Suk & Chemicals (Japan)	Reichold Chemicals	chemicals
Grand Metropolitan (UK)	Heublein, part of RJR–Nabisco and Pillsbury	wine and spirits diversified foods
Hachette (French)	Grolier	encyclopedias
Hanson Trust (UK)	Kidde	multi-industry
Hoechst (German)	Celanese	chemicals
L'Aire Liquide (French)	Big Three Industries	industrial gas
Nippon Mining (Japan)	Gould	electronics
Pechiney (France)	Triangle Industries	packaging
Sony (Japan)	CBS Records, part of CBS Corporation	audio, recording
Unilever (Netherlands and UK)	Chesebrough-Ponds	diversified consumer products

acquisitions in the United States by British, Canadian, French, German, and Japanese firms has cornered significant shares in specific industries and significantly increased foreign presence and leverage *vis-à-vis* American competition. A sample list of recent foreign acquisitions in the United States is shown in table 2.4.

Once stage four nears effective resolution, a drive for continued growth and economic power will propel big companies to the fifth stage, of acquiring less-related businesses. Here, Japanese and Korean firms, and possibly other Pacific superfirms, will be prepared to improve their global standings. They would begin with a uniquely demonstrated capacity for management of both size and complexity. So far, societal customs and international politics have acted to countermand the economics of such inter-industry diversification abroad. With time, however, the economic pressures should increase. For American industries that especially fit Japan's criteria of technology and capital intensiveness – like pharmaceuticals – entry by acquisition presents the most feasible alternative.

There is nothing pre-ordained about the sequence of international industrial development postulated above. In general, the early stages fit North American and European countries much better than Pacific Basin nations. In the final stages, however, the globalization of trade forces thinking in international terms and takes away the protective insulation of purely national strategies. The potential for inter-industry consolidations on a global scale is credible, if one accepts the underlying assumptions. Against that is an abiding faith in the value of specialized skills and the American way. If and when the validity of these latter assumptions are tested, the Japanese once again will be capable of springing a surprise. Being caught unprepared once by Japan is, perhaps, an understandable misreading of the rapid and unpredictable shifts in comparative advantage; short-sightedness a second time would be inexcusable.

Notes

1 William J. Baumol, *Business Behaviour, Value and Growth* (Macmillan, New York, 1959), p. 1.
2 George J. Stigler, *The Economist as Preacher* (University of Chicago Press, Chicago, 1982), p. 51. See also William J. Baumol, "Contestable markets, antitrust, and regulation," *Wharton*, 7 (Fall 1982), pp. 23–30, esp. p. 27.
3 Thomas J. Peters and Robert H. Waterman, Jr, *In Search of Excellence* (Harper & Row, New York, 1982).
4 Michael E. Porter, *Competitive Strategy: Techniques for Analyzing Industries and Competitors* (Free Press, New York, 1980); *Competitive Advantage: Creating and Sustaining Superior Performance* (Free Press, New York, 1985).
5 Edward S. Mason, "Price and production policies of large-scale enterprises," *American Economic Review*, 29 (1939), pp. 61–74; Joseph S. Bain, *Industrial Organization*, 2nd edn (Wiley, New York, 1968).
6 Michael E. Porter, "The contributions of industrial organization to strategic management," *Academy of Management Review*, 6 (1981), pp. 609–20, esp. p. 613.
7 Porter, *Competitive Advantage*, p. 7.
8 Walter Kiechel III, "Sniping at strategic planning," *Planning Review*, 12 (1984), p. 9. See also Vijay Mahajan and Yoram Wind, "Business strategy does not always pay off," *Long Range Planning*, 21 (1988), pp. 59–65.
9 Milton Leontiades, *Managing the Unmanageable: Strategies for Success within the Conglomerate* (Addison-Wesley, Reading, Mass., 1986).
10 Michael E. Porter, "From competitive advantage to corporate strategy," *Harvard Business Review* (1987), pp. 43–59, esp. p. 52.
11 *Forbes*, 13 July 1987, p. 145.
12 Porter, "From competitive advantage to corporate strategy," p. 46.
13 *Fortune*, May 1988, p. 46.

14 *Forbes*, 13 July 1987, p. 72.
15 Edith T. Penrose, *The Growth of the Firm* (Basil Blackwell, Oxford, 1972).
16 D. H. Robertson, *The Control of Industry*, 2nd edn (Nisbet, London, 1928), p. 85.
17 Adolph A. Berle, Jr, *The 20th Century Capitalist Revolution* (Harcourt Brace, New York, 1954), pp. 37–9.
18 Richard R. Ellsworth, "Subordinate financial policy to corporate strategy," *Harvard Business Review*, 61 (1983), p. 171.
19 Joel Stern, managing partner of the consulting firm of Stern, Stewart & Co; as quoted in *Planning Review*, 15 (1987), p. 43.
20 *Wall Street Journal*, 30 December 1987, p. 10.
21 Laszlo Birinyi, unpublished research study for Salomon Bros; as heard on "Wall Street Week," a weekly television business report, 9 January 1987.
22 *Fortune*, 12 September 1988, p. 140.
23 Ibid., p. 141.
24 *Wall Street Journal*, 31 August 1988, p. 49, and 31 August 1987, p. 10.
25 Gordon Donaldson and Jay Lorsch, *Decisioń Making at the Top: The Shaping of Strategic Direction* (Basic Books, New York, 1983), p. 8.
26 Oliver E. Williamson, *Markets and Hierarchies: Analysis and Antitrust Implications* (Macmillan, New York, 1975), esp. p. 162.
27 Adam Smith, *The Wealth of Nations*, as quoted in Walter Adams and James W. Brock, *The Bigness Complex* (Pantheon Books, New York, 1986), p. 229.
28 Adolf A. Berle and Gardiner C. Means, *The Modern Corporation and Private Property* (Harcourt Brace, New York, 1932).
29 Michael C. Jensen, "Takeovers: Folklore and science," *Harvard Business Review* (1984), pp. 109–20, esp. p. 109.
30 Andrew Hacker, *The Corporate Take-over* (Harper & Row, New York, 1964), p. 95. Also see Robert C. Clark, "Agency costs versus fiduciary duties," in *Principals and Agents: The Structure of Business*, eds Pratt and Zeckhauser (Harvard Business School Press, Boston, Mass., 1985), p. 57.
31 *Wall Street Journal*, 16 November 1987, p. 26.
32 A number of reviews of agency theory are readily available. A seminal article on this topic was written by Michael C. Jensen and William H. Meckling, "Theory of the firm: managerial behavior, agency costs and ownership structure," *Journal of Financial Economics*, 3 (1976), pp. 305–60.
33 Berle, *The 20th Century Capitalist Revolution*, p. 169.
34 Richard H. Pettway and Takeshi Yamada, "Mergers in Japan and their impact on shareholders' wealth," *Financial Management*, 15 (1986), pp. 43–52, esp. p. 44.
35 R. Shimizu, *The Growth of Firms in Japan* (Keio Tsushin, Tokyo, 1980); as quoted in Pettway and Yamada, "Mergers in Japan," p. 44.
36 Malcolm S. Salter and Wolf A. Weinhold, *Diversification through Acquisition* (Free Press, New York, 1979).
37 Porter, "From competitive advantage to corporate strategy," p. 46.
38 Alfred P. Sloan, Jr, *My Years with General Motors* (Doubleday, New York, 1964), p. xxii.
39 *Forbes*, 15 September 1967, p. 230.
40 Peters and Waterman, *In Search of Excellence*.
41 Porter, "From competitive advantage to corporate strategy," p. 47.
42 A quote of Ennius Bergsma, partner in the international consulting firm of McKinsey; as mentioned in *Fortune*, 25 April 1988, p. 60.

43 Porter, "From competitive advantage to corporate strategy," p. 55.
44 Ibid., p. 49.
45 Ibid., p. 52.
46 Organization for Economic Co-operation and Development, "The industrial policy of Japan," p. 15; as quoted in Thomas K. McCraw, *America versus Japan* (Harvard Business School Press, Boston, Mass., 1986), p. 9.
47 Alfred D. Chandler, Jr and Herman Daems, eds, *Managerial Hierarchies* (Harvard University Press, Cambridge, Mass., 1980), Introduction, p. 4.
48 Herman H. Trachsel, *Public Utilities Regulation* (Irwin, Chicago, 1947), pp. 396, 398.
49 Chandler and Daems, *Managerial Hierarchies*, p. 3.
50 Jay B. Barney and William G. Ouchi, eds, *Organizational Economics* (Jossey-Bass, San Francisco, Calif., 1986), p. 160.
51 Williamson, *Markets and Hierarchies*, see esp. ch. on "multidivisional structure."
52 *Wall Street Journal*, 12 May 1988, p. 58.
53 *Fortune*, 25 April 1988, p. 60. Citing the work of Stephen Coley, partner in the international consulting firm of McKinsey.
54 *Forbes*, 16 May 1988, p. 86.
55 Ibid., p. 88.

3
Diversification Demythified

Myths, either singly or in combination, have served to insulate theory from reality. As artifices, they have deflected attention from the real work of management in order to further an alternative image that is more amenable to scientific methodology. The essential goal of positive science, according to John Neville Keynes, the authority relied upon by Milton Friedman when he developed his views of "positive economics," is the "investigation of *uniformities*."[1] This places the emphasis on the internal consistency of relationships. Indeed, applications in economics can be extremely limited. Nevertheless, no matter how thin the slice of reality under investigation, it is treated as bona fide and preferable to an explanation with greater practical appeal, but one that is indeterminate in terms of matching causes with effects. This structured approach has led to precise, but very narrow and circumscribed views of business: for example, perfect competition. This technique is admissible as long as the limitations are kept in mind. It is important to remember, as Keynes pointed out, that a "scientific" hypothesis is chosen "because it is the simplest, and not because it is the nearest to the facts."[2]

The ability of a hypothesis to shed light on the "what is" of business, therefore, is only as good as the realism of the "facts" from which it is derived. Milton Friedman is careful in distinguishing between "what is" and "what should be" in his treatise on *Positive Economics*. Based on definitions borrowed from John Neville Keynes, Friedman points out that the first obligation of positive science is in finding *regularities* and that general applications are neither a direct concern nor obligation of an economic theory. The "what is" of perfect competition, for example, is extremely limited to a very tiny corner of the universe. Outside the agricultural markets, the favorite textbook illustration used to demonstrate how the principle of the "invisible hand" of the marketplace *might* work, one is hard put to find a single practical example in use. "What is" in terms of relevance for the practice of business is virtually unexplored.

In studying the "what is" that concerns business managers, and that therefore should concern students of business management, it is necessary to clear the air of "what isn't." Progress in advancing the state of knowledge about management in order to improve the performance of managers cannot succeed if it is continually sidetracked by diversionary arguments devised with a totally different objective in mind. The myths in chapter 2 are six such diversions. They are used in one guise or another to prop up hypothetical models of firm behavior. They obstruct the direct investigation of firms: how they are managed, how they compete with one another, and what motivates them to take actions different from each other. Myths preserve "old" beliefs. They keep the past alive. Specifically, myths contribute to three dominant themes around which current teachings of firm behavior still evolve.

Three Mythical Notions of the Firm

Management is Powerless (Classical Economic Theory)

Until relatively recently, the entire thrust of economic orthodoxy centered on the importance of impersonal supply and demand forces in the marketplace and the helplessness of individual decision-makers to influence the market's outcomes. Even as firms and institutions gain greater size and standing, they are seen as *relatively* small and inconsequential in the larger scheme of total economic activity. When perfect competition was originally formulated as the economist's way of simplifying and depicting business conduct, the truly small and individually powerless merchant owners were indeed helpless in the face of collective market forces.

In the classical market system, resource allocation does not require the conscious exercise of management's discretion. Indeed, under the simplifying assumptions of certainty and complete information, there is no role for management to fill. The firm is merely a processing station, receiving "orders" from the market and producing "outputs" in response. Managers only contribute peripherally to this process: they are necessary in a supervisory sense, but primarily they act as unthinking agents that carry out instructions received from the marketplace.

Moreover, as conceived, classical economic doctrine treats production as a specialized process in the output of a single product. The doctrine of specialization does not explicitly allow for multi-product firms, or diversification beyond a one-product focus. Strictly speaking, neither multi-product nor multi-business firms can be explained by reference to classical economic theory, and therefore none of the efficiencies inherent in the classicist's "theory of the firm" are applicable to diversification.

Management is an Agent for Shareholders (Neoclassical Economic/ Finance View)

Over time, the symmetry of interests that applied when owners were also managers no longer typified large and growing public corporations. The separation of the functions of ownership and management in these organizations now is impossible to ignore. It forces an explanation of how the two parties, although divided, cooperate for the common objective of firm efficiency.

In a clever conceptualization, a so-called theory of agency postulates that managers and owners are bound together as contractual partners, with shareowners delegating orders to their agents, the managers. In effect, nothing much changes under these assumptions. Firms and their managers are as inconsequential as before. The firm merely acts as a "nexus" in facilitating the bringing together of buyers and sellers in market-like transactions. In this way, the "behavior of the firm is like the behavior of the market."[3]

Looked at from a principal–agent relationship, managers are obligated to further the interests of the firm's shareholders and legal owners. Since this implicit contract would not be self-enforcing if managers were left on their own – to pursue their personal goals – the capital market is crucial as the instrument for assuring that management complies with its contractual obligation to shareowners. Should managers not obey the wishes of a firm's shareowners, then shareowners can oust the managers by voting them out of office. Threats of a takeover are also a discipline exerted through the capital markets, presumably ensuring that managers will act in the best interests of their shareowners.

But what is in the shareowners' best interests? Economists never bother to ask or investigate this question directly. In agency theory, economists presume to speak for shareholders. Unsurprisingly, what economists have shareowners believing is exactly what economists themselves believe.

Diversification, for example, fares no better under agency theory than it does in the theory of perfect competition. Two arguments basically are employed against diversification. Both look at diversification as a shareowner prerogative rather than as a managerial decision, and, in both, actions are guided by an abiding faith in the desirability of specialization and the concomitant disadvantages of diversification.

Argument 1. Because shareowners can diversify their investments among different companies, managers need not bother diversifying for them. Management's job is to "stick to its knitting." Put more strongly, the advantages of specialization dictate against firms diversifying, because that would jeopardize the efficiency attributed to specialization. Thus, the independent status of shareowners is used to reinforce the conventional case for firm specialization. Also, the supposition that capital markets enforce an agent–principal relationship is consistent with the hypothesis that markets rather than individuals and institutions make decisions.

Argument 2. Shareowners' interests are protected through actions in the capital market. If managers pursue less than efficient strategies, share prices drop and remedial actions follow. The ultimate remedy is the takeover of the firm and firing of management. Shareowners, in essence, keep management "on track" by exercising their voting power to enforce their collective will. Although this does not directly address the question of diversification, multi-business firms or conglomerates are portrayed as the logical targets for disciplinary action, since they stray furthest from a close-knit business specialization. The market for capital now serves an important second function as a market for corporate control that can be used to discipline those companies that fail to pursue efficiency in operations. Starting with a conviction that specialization is an optimum strategy, the implication is that the further afield a firm ventures, the more likely it is to find itself the target of a takeover attempt or other corrective action.

Management's Actions are "Bounded" (Industrial Organization View)

An adaptation of the economic framework of industrial organization provides a third popular guide to how managers might strategize. Originally, industrial organization economics concerned itself with how organizations functioned within given industry structures and how their actions contributed to the public welfare. As updated, primarily in Michael Porter's writings, traditional industrial organization assumptions are modified, but the theme of operating within fixed industry boundaries is only slightly relaxed.

Because industrial organization economics takes the position that companies are rooted deeply in their product markets, there is no need for a corporate-level orientation. Corporations are essentially perceived as the sum of the operating units that comprise them. Further, industrial organization does not abandon the economist's goal of efficiency gains through specialization and cost reduction, so that decisions by firms in diversifying away from their core business lie outside the domain of industrial organization.

By accepting these assumptions on specialization and industry stability (except for limited cases where the use of specialized skills or resources makes "related" diversification feasible), Porter sees management strategy as bound by the confines of a company's core business. In combining relative industry stability with an economist's belief in specialization,

Porter has little choice but to counsel management to "stick to its knitting."

Whereas the departure from industrial organization economics appears dramatic on the surface, Porter primarily refurbishes an old standard. By depending on the existing structure of markets to largely determine firm conduct, the firm once again is rendered impotent to chart a future course much different from its past, and its managers are only able to act strategically in dealing with operational problems of a business-unit level.

None of the three portrayals above gives a satisfactory picture of the "what is" of business. By design, none takes the business firm as the primary object of analysis. Each starts from an intellectual bias that looks to markets instead of firms, or to shareholders rather than managers, in order to explain firm behavior. The first duty is to methodology. If you have a hammer, you look for nails. If mathematics and statistics are your tools, you seek closed-loop solutions. The choice of methodology also dictates a set of limiting assumptions, with statics the most conforming climate for the use of quantitative analysis.

In sum, if one is oriented to "model" problem-solving, then stability or predictability of relationships is crucial. On the other hand, if change is the expected state of affairs, then the orientation is toward a flexible and adaptable frame of thinking. What is important, therefore, is whether stability or change is more relevant for modern capitalism. If the latter is more characteristic, then "scientific" methods cannot explain enough.

Three Periods of Major Industry Change

To test the accuracy of the standard assumption of relative market stability, three critical periods in shaping modern American business are surveyed below. In each period, dramatic changes occurred to alter the course of business development. An investigation of the events, however brief, is helpful in explaining the transitions from small single-business, single-product firms to the complex giant corporations of today.

1898–1903

Within a relatively short span of years around the turn of the century, a number of giant enterprises were formed in massive simultaneous consolidations of competitors. During the six years from 1898 to 1903, more than two thousand firms were absorbed by merger. About 1,200 disappeared in 1899 alone.[4] Combinations created to control a majority share of industry output were the genesis of companies like American Brands, International Harvester (now Navistar), International Paper, United States Steel,

General Electric, DuPont, American Can, Otis Elevator, and Pittsburgh Plate Glass. These consolidations of power were the result of companies seeking to escape the effects of competition, while gaining the advantage of market control.

When the first manufacturers engaged in mass production, markets were opening and demand was expanding. Anticipating future growth, producers borrowed capital to build even larger facilities, adding to fixed costs and constructing specialized assets suited only for particular production processes. By the 1870s, a vibrant financial system was able and eager to supply the capital to keep American industry growing. Having geared up for growth, the burgeoning industrial system relied on continued expansion for a satisfactory return on the productive capacity that had been built. Burdened by high interest costs, managements needed to keep mass-production facilities utilized

The economic crises in 1873 and 1893 exposed the vulnerability of manufacturers to an unbridled, cut-throat fight for markets and profits. Prompted to take counter-measures, producers tried to "manage" competition through a series of pools, trusts, and holding-company arrangements. The first of these attempts, a voluntary agreement among competing producers to "pool" profits, was unenforceable and ineffective, due to widespread cheating by the pool's members. As a substitute, trusts were organized; these had the advantage over pools of vesting authority in a board of trustees who controlled the separate operating companies that comprised the trust and acted as its stockholders. Holding companies superseded trusts in a legal maneuver to avoid the growing antitrust sentiments and legislative calls for reform.

The Northern Securities Case of 1904 was the legal test case that successfully halted future combinations, regardless of the nature of the arrangement, formed for the express purpose of eliminating competition. The Northern Securities Company acted as a holding company for three large railroads that had been financed and merged by the nation's most notorious railroad tycoons and finance capitalists. Ruled in restraint of trade, the court ordered the Northern Securities combine to be broken up, with its dismantlement serving as the stimulus for the eventual split-up of the Standard Oil Company and the American Tobacco Company.

The multi-merger movement came to an abrupt end. Although individual acquisitions continued, with a build-up of acquisition activity in the 1920s and beyond, the "consolidation era" of multiple horizontal mergers had come to a close.

Concurrent with the rise of pools, trusts, and holding companies, "merger promoters" came into their own. J. P. Morgan, the greatest financier of his day, engineered some of the most formidable combinations: for example, AT&T, International Harvester, General Electric, Pullman, Western

Union, and Westinghouse. Each company dominated or was a powerful force in its industry. Best remembered for the creation of the first $1 billion, corporation – the United States Steel Corporation – J. P. Morgan was the first among a select group of financial promoters who encouraged and profited handsomely from corporate restructurings.

Eventually, financial promoters turned the reins of corporate control back to management. J. P. Morgan and his cohorts were never concerned with permanent jobs in management; their interest was not economic efficiency, but financial gain. They captured the opportunity to employ capital creatively by supplying needed financing and by offering large above-market premiums for companies to relinquish control. The pattern to J. P. Morgan's strategy, for example, remained essentially unchanged: simplify the organizational structure, recapitalize, link small lines into a larger system, and put Morgan's managers in control.[5]

After the Northern Securities Company decision, the influence of J. P. Morgan and the Wall Street banking houses progressively declined. Nevertheless, their indelible imprint remained, and major industry concentrations, once formed, tended to persist. The resulting recasting of power bases appeared so permanent that historians expected the industry structures so created to endure throughout most of the twentieth century.

1950s–1960s

The mid-1950s marked the second grand revolution in American industry, typified by so-called "conglomerate" restructuring. Upsetting a period of relative industry stability, conglomerates represented a new way to grow. Guided by strong company managers, these new types of corporate structures arose as a result of acquisitions made in seemingly unconnected businesses across a number of different industries. The emphasis on unrelated acquisitions defied the conventional tactic of trying for greater specialization within a single industry and effectively bypassed antitrust legislation drafted only with that contingency in mind.

A common trait of the new conglomerates was an emphasis on "financial engineering." Instead of running a business according to product specialization, the emphasis was on the management of capital. The conglomerate capitalist's blueprint led him to wherever the returns on capital appeared highest. The stratagem often resulted in a strange assemblage of corporate parts, mixing manufacturing, mining, agriculture, and service firms indiscriminately.

Conglomerates were closely identified with the entrepreneurs who built them: Jimmy Ling of LTV, Harold Geneen of IT&T, Charles Bluhdorn of Gulf & Western, Henry Singleton of Teledyne, Charles Thornton and Roy Ash of Litton, and George Strichman of Colt Industries. Each person leveraged a small beginning into a giant organization or else took a lethargic, slow-growing firm as the vehicle for diversification. A trademark of the early conglomerates was a dizzying array of combinations, pieced together by equally imaginative uses of financing. Conglomerate managers were not afraid to exceed industry norms for debt, with high borrowings justified on the basis of expected high returns from acquired businesses.

The acknowledged "father" of the conglomerate movement was Royal Little, the founder and chief executive of the Textron Corporation. His inauspicious beginning in the textile business during the 1920s and 1930s was given a boost during the Second World War by orders from the defense department for parachute materials and jungle hammocks. After the war, when Little switched his unused mill capacity in defense orders to produce consumer goods, he conceived a strategy for building a new kind of company.

First, he got bigger by buying a number of textile firms very cheaply. A glut of old New England textile mills, together with aging owners eager to sell, gave Little the opportunity to acquire many firms below their net worth. By the mid-1950s, Little was ready to move beyond textiles by buying a maker of airborne antennas and a producer of testing equipment. Soon after, he acquired the one large remaining textile producer in northeast America: the American Woolen Company. Within a year, Little had acquired five other companies. Pursuing this pattern of opportunistic buying, Little's acquisition of Bell Aircraft cost just $32 million in 1962; a transaction considered as an expensive miscalculation at the time, but which proved enormously profitable and far-sighted in retrospect. Following Litttle's strategy, Textron became a multi-business corporation by combining Bell Aircraft (helicopters) with Homelite (chainsaws), CWC (iron castings), Bridgeport (milling machines), Camcar (fasteners), Fafnir (bearings), Jacobsen (lawn mowers), and Sheaffer Eaton (stationery).

Royal Little's conglomerate strategy soon spread. Buoyed by a rising stock market, entrepreneurs saw a way for quick financial gains. In stock-for-stock swaps of securities, for example, companies with high price-to-earnings ratios could acquire firms with lower-priced earnings at a favorable exchange rate. As long as such stock-swap opportunities existed, corporations could continue showing earnings gains without generating any greater efficiencies from actually improving the operation of the businesses they had acquired. What seemed a new formula for creating instant wealth, however, proved no substitute in the end for careful planning and sound management.

Encouraged by Wall Street financiers and management consultants, both eager to participate in the rewards from offering advice on the new strategy of diversification, the collective ambitions of corporation entrepreneurs exceeded their ability to manage the enterprises they had so hastily assembled. Those conglomerates built without an operational rationale or strategy in mind were susceptible to a worsening in the economic climate and deteriorating operating efficiencies. During the 1970s, the combined effects of slowing economic growth, a sagging stock market, burdensome debt, and limited managerial capacity forced the divestiture of many companies purchased just a few years earlier.

However, although the success of individual conglomerates proved to be transitory, the strategy itself has made a lasting imprint. Just as the horizontal merger movement before it, the conglomerate movement left its mark. Following an initial burst of experimentation, the concept of unrelated diversification was eventually accepted by large blue-chip organizations that had at first merely watched the tactics of Little, Ling, Bluhdorn, Geneen, and others from the sidelines. Even if no further conglomerate acquisitions are made – an unlikely forecast – the strategy of unrelated diversification will have made a lasting impression on the structure of the nation's industries.

The 1980s

The third wave of industry restructuring accentuated the role of the individual entrepreneur. T. Boone Pickens was among the first of this new entrepreneurial breed who used unfriendly takeover threats to force managements into either facing the prospect of losing the company in a proxy battle or taking action to raise the share price in order to win the backing of its shareholders.

One distinguishing aspect in this era was the sheer magnitude of the deals. Companies that had been traditionally thought to be untouchable, simply because of the enormous capital required to buy them, became the targets of individual investors who were amply supplied with capital by eager financial backers. In 1984 and 1985, T. Boone Pickens attempted his first mega-deals: Gulf and Unocal, two oil giants. Although unsuccessful in purchasing either firm, Pickens made a profit of over $200 million and $80 million respectively from his "unsuccessful" tenders. Once the feasibility of the strategy had been tested, a number of other entrepreneurial raiders joined in the newest version of corporate gamesmanship.

Among those who became the best-known deal-makers were Carl Icahn, Irwin Jacobs, Asher Edelman, Ronald Perlman, Sir James Goldsmith, the Bass brothers, and the Belzberg brothers. With one or two exceptions (notably Icahn's purchase of TWA airlines and Ronald Perlman's acquisition of Revlon, a leading cosmetics maker), this group succeeded in profiting from investing rather than managing. The typical ploy was to accumulate a minor stock position in a targeted company before announcing an intention to make an offer for control at a price substantially above the current stock market quote. Management's reflex reaction was to fend off the uninvited suitor, by buying up the shares already purchased, if possible, or adopting defensive measures known as "poison pills," including the sale of assets, repurchase of stock, acquiring other companies, or a variety of legal maneuvers. If all else failed, management often looked for a friendly acquirer, a "white knight" more to its liking and who would let existing managers keep their jobs.

By 1988, the US economy was enjoying its sixth year without a recession. Financial institutions were extremely liquid and anxiously seeking profitable outlets for their funds. The rapid and immensely profitable transactions negotiated by "private raiders" like Pickens, Icahn, etc. encouraged others to try their hand at corporate takeovers. The next stage of deal-making involved partnerships formed by several individuals in order to do "leveraged buyouts" (LBOs). In a typical leveraged buyout, the first step is familiar: find a company whose stock is selling substantially below its estimated realizable value. After purchase, the new managers either recover their investment by selling off all the company's assets or, more often, they emphasize cash management, which generally requires some asset sales plus very stringent cost-containment measures such as sharp cutbacks in expenditures, research and development, and reduction in employee and management staffing levels. The trademarks of a typical leveraged buyout follow a pattern: the acquired firm takes on massive debt, requiring large interest payments and an orientation on short-term results.

Where the partners engaged in leveraged buyouts differ from the earlier financial speculators in this period is in assuming control of the companies. Once purchased, a company is placed under the management of the leveraged buyout group. A professional manager is hired, but the key decisions rest firmly with the partners of the leveraged buyout. In a sense, these partners emulate the late J. P. Morgan: they build business combinations, with a financier's rather than an industrialist's philosophy. The aim is the implementation of a new way to make money through control of companies, followed by restructuring, severe cost-cutting, and asset sales.

Fueling the leveraged buyout movement is access to capital. In 1988, an estimated $100 billion was available for commitment to new deals.[6] Traditionally, a deal is initiated by a relatively minor contribution by the leveraged buyout group, say 1 percent of the total purchase price. Other passive investors such as banks and insurance firms put up the majority of the funds. Increasingly, pension funds are also sponsors in leverage buyout pools. Thus, with a minimum personal stake, a leveraged buyout partnership can quickly put together the financing to undertake transactions of even the largest domestic corporations. The leader among this new type of investor is Kohlberg Kravis Roberts. Latecomers, but extremely well-

Table 3.1 The fifteen largest US leveraged buyouts: 1981–8

Target company (parent)	Investor group	Amount ($ billions)
RJR–Nabisco	Kohlberg Kravis Roberts	25.0+
Beatrice	Kohlberg Kravis Roberts	6.2
Borg–Warner	Merrill Lynch Capital	4.7
Southland	Salomon Bros and Goldman Sachs	4.6
Safeway Stores	Kohlberg Kravis Roberts	4.3
Montgomery Ward (Mobil)	GE Capital and Kidder Peabody	3.8
R. H. Macy	Goldman Sachs	3.7
Owens–Illinois	Kohlberg Kravis Roberts	3.6
Viacom International	National Amusements	3.4
Burlington Industries	Morgan Stanley	2.6
Storer Communications	Kohlberg Kravis Roberts	2.5
American Standard	Kelso	2.5
Jim Walter	Kohlberg Kravis Roberts	2.4
Lear Siegler	Forstmann Little	2.1
Colt Industries	Morgan Stanley	2.0

financed competitors, include the Wall Street firms of Morgan Stanley and Merrill Lynch. Table 3.1 lists some of the former public companies that were purchased by prominent leveraged buyout groups.

A leveraged buyout of a company may also be engineered by management, sometimes with the help of an LBO-led syndicate; such a buyout leaves the company intact after the transaction, except that the former hired managers are now major owners. Recent illustrations of large companies that have recapitalized and gone private include Macy's, the department-store chain, and Southland, operator of the largest chain of convenience stores in the USA. In both cases, managements' actions were prompted by the threat of an unfriendly tender offer. In these cases, it is up to the same managements to squeeze out greater efficiencies – defined as the ability to meet its much greater financial obligations, while remaining competitive – than when it operated as a public company.

Also, public corporations have initiated their own restructuring, in an urgency to move before action from outside the company is imposed on them. Holiday Corporation, for example, rather than capitulate to investor–developer Donald Trump's attempt at control, chose to restructure itself, selling off many of its hotel properties, making a hefty payment to shareholders, and assuming a tremendous debt burden in the process.

Finally, senior management of RJR–Nabisco, in a proposed mega-deal, initiated a move to take the company private through a leveraged buyout.

The intent was to free the company's top management from the normal scrutiny and criticisms that any large public company attracts, while significantly raising the value of RJR–Nabisco in the process, and coincidentally conferring enormous potential wealth on a few top managers. As part of the arrangement, RJR–Nabisco contemplated selling off part of its businesses in order to pay off the enormous debt required to finance the leveraged buyout. As it turned out, the company's board of directors accepted an offer for the company made by Kohlberg Kravis Roberts to management's bid. This latest era of restructuring is still continuing. Following precedent, it will take a sharp business contraction or major legislation to bring it to an end. Whatever the future brings, however, the industrial landscape will never be the same. An unprecedented series of company acquisitions, divestitures, asset sales, and redefinition of business focus have realigned the competitive features of major industries for ever: oil, soft drink, department stores, food, cosmetics, and textiles are just some of the industry sectors affected.

Another trademark of this period has been the renewal of horizontal merger and acquisition activity. A relaxed antitrust attitude toward bigness has encouraged large companies to purchase major competitors. In fact, the second major round of consolidations within industry sectors in this century has gone almost unnoticed. Acquisition proposals that in the past would have aroused vigorous protest from the Justice Department have proceeded unhindered. Virtually free of legal restraints, companies have moved aggressively in reshuffling the competitive make-up of industry after industry.

If there is a theme to this third wave, it is the simple drive for profits. There is no unifying operational motif. Building bigger one-purpose enterprises to achieve greater efficiencies, or merging different firms into conglomerate superfirms, as in previous major restructurings, are not driving this round of change. All firms, in whatever industry, qualify as potential takeovers. The acid test is simply the current market valuation of a firm's stock relative to an estimate of its value in a takeover. Assuming the arithmetic works out, what the company makes or what industry it is in is of little consequence. In many ways, the approach is reminiscent of the earlier conglomerate strategy with assortments of companies controlled by leveraged buyout partners that are often more random than the typical conglomerate (see table 3.2). In this instance, however, individual investors rather than corporations are the buyers, and they lack the administrative structure for coordinating the separate businesses.

Loosely administered under a holding-company arrangement, each acquired business that is controlled by a leveraged buyout partnership stands on its own, so to speak, with no sharing of interests except that of ownership. The time-span of leveraged buyout control is typically a few

Table 3.2 Companies controlled by financial managers (*c.* 1988)

Controller	Selected companies controlled
Kohlberg Kravis Roberts	Dillingham Fred Meyer Motel 6 Owens–Illinois Stop & Shop Jim Walter RJR–Nabisco
Merrill Lynch Capital	Amstar Borg–Warner Jack Eckerd Supermarkets General
Morgan Stanley Group	Burlington Industries Container Corporation of America Sterling Chemical

years, or enough time to make the business sufficiently attractive to be remarketed, either in a public or private sale. No synergy is contemplated, in the conventional sense. Whereas a 1950s-style conglomerate may strive to make two plus two equal to five by operating firms more efficiently in combination than they were operated as separate entities, a leveraged buyout–conglomerate resembles a mutual fund that makes stock investments, except that its portfolio consists of actual companies with new companies added as earlier purchases are sold. In principle, this type of holding-company arrangement can grow infinitely large. It would probably shock the average person to realize that the revenues of the companies under the control of Kohlberg Kravis Roberts's leveraged buyout partnership in 1987 totaled about $38 billion, $1 billion larger than the sales of General Electric, the sixth largest company on *Fortune* magazine's list of the 500 largest industrial companies.

A Perspective on Historical Change

Each of the three historic movements above changed business in fundamental ways. However, the impetus for change, and the specific manner in which businesses would be affected, could not be predicted. In each instance, an open-market system was the enabling mechanism. It created opportunities for entrepreneurs visionary enough, and with an innovative flair, to do things better or in a different manner than they had been done before. As in the past, whenever "experts" have despaired that the future holds no new surprises, an unexpected surge of renewal has proved the prediction to be premature.[7]

Seeing change as normal rather than exceptional is of course the way Schumpeter characterized a dynamic society. He foresaw "waves of creative destruction" as endemic. Rather than being harmful, disruptions were necessary in revitalizing the system and moving it toward new and advanced levels of industry progress. Schumpeter knew that stability was a prescription for economic decline; yet change was incompatible with the tenets of classical economics. The economic community clung to statics in order to preserve its claim on being a positive science. By assuming "static equilibrium" as the normal state of affairs, a study of the dynamics of change was obviated. Economists had to settle for explanations of existing systems at a given point in time, even though they could not explain logically how one system had led to the next and were ideologically incapable of contemplating any further change.

Paradoxically, the very "openness" of markets that underlies classical economics also contributes to the instability of the entire system. Economics, in effect, has developed a theoretical logic at odds with itself. It works best when freedom of firm and individual intiatives and choices are at a minimum. Yet this is directly contrary to the objective of competitive efficiency, whereby all market participants are free to try and maximize their respective positions.

What the economic community omitted, even consciously suppressed, was the concept of entrepreneurship: the idea that differences among individual firm managers and their conduct of businesses could influence overall market behavior. Ironically, a banker and economist by the name of Richard Cantillon was credited with introducing the word "entrepreneur." In the example he used, Cantillon associated entrepreneurs with the risk-taking involved in buying land holdings at one price with the purpose of selling at a later date at a higher price. Jean-Baptiste Say, a famous French economist, applied Cantillon's idea to the risk-taking involved in running a business, using Say's own practical business background in banking, insurance, and textiles to extend Cantillon's original version. Schumpeter, at the age of 28, in his PhD thesis "The Theory of Economic Development", outlined the prominent role played by "creative entrepreneurship." For Schumpeter, it was *the* principal force for economic growth.

Before publishing his doctoral treatise, Schumpeter had been a lawyer and finance minister in his native Austria. Thus, the three economists most closely identified with advocating the importance of the entrepreneur drew from personal experience. In common with other early economics writers, their exposure to business shaped the way they saw and wrote about business affairs.

This outward-looking approach to economics, however, is not tractable with the mechanics of modern economics. As the economics profession moved inexorably to embrace stability, it had to abandon Schumpeterian-style dynamism. Moreover, the idea that entrepreneurs could stand out and make a difference was inconsistent with the classical assumption of a market-driven economy that, by definition, could not be influenced by anyone within it. There was no choice but to expunge the idea of entrepreneurship from the mainstream of economic studies. At present, it can be categorically said that "there is no established economic theory of the entrepreneur. The subject area has been surrendered by economists to sociologists, psychologists, and political scientists. Indeed, almost all the social sciences have a theory of the entrepreneur, except economics."[8]

Although mention of entrepreneurs may be omitted from textbooks, their impact on business cannot. Each of the three cycles of restructuring in this century was instigated by entrepreneurs. Whether centered around the actions of a J. P. Morgan, Royal Little, T. Boone Pickens, or Kohlberg Kravis Roberts, the spark for change came not from tradition-bound managers, but from those determined to upset the normal bureaucratic routine.

In each episode, the enabling tactic was a transfer of control. J. P. Morgan bought companies in order to stifle competition by controlling markets. Morgan was willing to pay handsomely in order to realize the potential profits from combining many companies into single large organizations that could act as price-setters for their industry. Royal Little built his conglomerate empire by acquiring many dissimilar firms whose managements were receptive to being bought out at the "right" price and where passive shareholders offered no resistance. In the late-1980s phase of restructuring, control has often been wrested from management's grip, either through hostile proxy fights, unsolicited tender offers, or as a last-ditch surrender of a company to a "white knight" – the lesser evil, when loss of control seemed inescapable.

In times of radical change, traditional managements have given way to entrepreneurial managements. This, in turn, has been prevalent only since about the last quarter of the nineteenth century, with the separation of ownership from management and the emergence of financial markets that enabled shares in companies to be readily transferred from one owner to another. The transferability of ownership interests created a new dimension to the conventional view of stock markets as merely suppliers of equity capital. With an efficient new mechanism for shifting corporate control, waves of "creative destruction" threaten any and all publicly-held companies, with adverse implications for the credibility of a theory based on statics and an impassive marketplace. Adolph Berle, who posed the rhetorical question "Who owns American business?" has yet to receive a definitive answer.

There can be little doubt that further struggles for control of American businesses lie ahead. Only a small percentage of voting power rests with corporate managers. Of the remainder, pension funds account for a lion's share. Private pension plans of corporations account for about two-thirds of the total pension assets, which are in excess of $1 trillion, with about half of that amount invested in stocks of US companies.

Potential control has seldom remained unused for long. A more active and independent involvement by pension funds in the affairs of the companies they own is predictable, although the exact course and timing of their actions are unknown. According to one account, based on a letter dated February 23, 1988 from the US Labor Department to Avon Products, the long-standing policy of restraint by trustees of pension plans will be replaced by "a new brand of shareholder activism." Guidelines prompting trustees to concern themselves with economic consequences, coupled with provisions of personal liability, should mean that "more corporate pension plans will start to vote against those management-sheltering poison pills that have the effect of lowering the value of shares . . . [with the undoubted effect] that private pension plans will start to act as owners of stock, not just as traders of stock."[9]

The shift in the locus of control promises to alter permanently the privileged situation of management to have both freedom to manage and freedom to control. The loss of an automatic mandate for management from its shareowners means that the functions of ownership and management must be evaluated separately from the personal motives of each party. Although a division in principle has existed for many years, the wide dispersion of voting power and lack of a unified shareholder voice gave management *de facto* powers of command in the past. With the concentration of shares in institutional hands, the ability to influence managements, or remove managements altogether, injects an unpredictable element of future change in the traditional relationship between managers and shareholders, and reaffirms Schumpeter's notion of continuous *disequilibrium*.

Towards a New View of the Driving Forces for Change

Although change is continuous, it tends to vary in intensity from time to time. An uninterrupted string of restructuring and reorganizing would give no pause for harvesting the gains of reform. Businesses tend to alternate between rapid cycles of change and assimilation, revolution and evolution.

The highest peaks in this progression are the most uncertain in terms of predictability and are characterized by a trial-and-error style of management. During the radical restructurings described earlier, the processes began tentatively, with entrepreneurs groping to establish the logical parameters in a bold new strategy.

Adopting a new corporate philosophy is never as smooth, orderly, and error-free as a purely rational decision-model implies. Accordingly, the types of managers appropriate for revolutionary and evolutionary transitions tend to be divided along these two lines of emphasis. When companies are gradually evolving, between periods of rapid transformation, then managements can be thought of as being in a relatively "steady-state" mode,[10] demanding no more in the way of management skills than a competent professional manager might normally be expected to deliver. On the other hand, when a company is leaving one stage of growth for another, it needs creative managers able to deal with the uncertain and transitional nature of such a strategy.

Individual companies can persist in a steady-state condition, even during periods punctuated by change. In the late 1980s, for example, many companies evolved normally and gradually, even during the most dramatic industry-wide restructuring of the century. There is no lock-step pattern to the seasons of change for particular firms. The stimulus for leaving an evolutionary path may be forced from without, as in new environmental pressures, or introduced from within by a new corporate management along with a new entrepreneurial spirit.

During times of great stress, rational strategic models are seldom of much assistance. Having not yet experienced what is to come, and being unable to predict the duration or nature of change, managements are left largely on their own instincts and backgrounds to work through the actions necessary for their survival and growth. Once new patterns of behavior are adapted and routinized, strategic advice can then be formulated that allows organizations that follow to learn and imitate the lessons of experience. It is in this arena that strategy and business policy are largely forced to operate. The underlying, constant movements of history can be studied and used to anticipate the appropriate courses of future action. Persistent currents will continue moving companies along an evolutionary scale, in other words, despite occasional gusts or gales that temporarily drive them in unexpected and unpredictable directions.

Different styles of management provide the missing conceptual link for the dynamics of change. The transition from a single- to a multi-business organization, for example, suggests a shift in management philosophy to implement the reorientation in strategy. Yet no formal model of strategic management incorporates more than a single dimension of management, despite the dissimilarities in strategy.

Once more, Schumpeter has anticipated the exigencies of strategy. Long before it became popular to talk of managerial "types," Schumpeter proposed a distinction between "creative" and "adaptive" managers. Creative managers are those who make an impact on an entire business system, or at least a significant part of it, whereas the adaptive personality tends to the normal administrative responsibilities of running a business. For present-day circumstances, a more apt distinction might be between "controllers" and "administrators." The former assume control during transitionary stages. Controllers lack the intimate business knowledge of an administrative manager. The basic orientation of controllers also differs, stressing a financial and short-term view concentrated in a brief, but dynamic reign of command.

Controllers seek to restructure. Whether at the turn of the century or nearly ninety years later, the drive of the controller has been to capture the abnormal rewards from acquiring control, adopting a new corporate-level strategy, and seeking a propitious time to leave the business. The first-movers in innovating a new strategy take the greatest risks and, if successful, reap extraordinary rewards. The huge profits generally attract additional participants, from Wall Street, management consultancy firms, and independent financial promoters. The very success of the movement causes it to expand and extend and eventually to hemorrhage from its excesses. Invariably, a pattern is followed: innovation, imitation, and speculation. The cycle generally ends with, or leads to the passage of, legislation designed to curb the extremes to which the original idea is stretched.

In economics, the profit motive is assumed to push companies to compete and excel. This same profiteering motive drives individual entrepreneurs as well. When the economy is flush with liquid pools of capital, as it was in the mid-1980s, a tremendous pressure builds to innovate ways to channel it into new ventures. Within the limits of the legal system, entrepreneurs strain for ever more creative devices to "outsmart" the system. Momentum for leveraged buyouts, for instance, was propelled by just such a combination of money and motive.

In order to understand the implications of creative restructurings, the motives of "controllers," as distinct from "administrators," have to be appreciated. Generally, controllers stand in stark contrast to professional managers, both in demeanor and style. They have no attachment to the institutions they seek to control. Preserving a company's structure intact – the instinct for corporate survival that is foremost in a traditional manager's list of concerns – is often inimical to the controller's fixation on a rapid creation of wealth. As one head of a leveraged buyout put it, managers have to realize "they're no longer building an empire – they're building money."[11]

Also, firm "efficiency," as it is commonly understood, may be an indirect by-product of a controller's actions, but it is not the pimary objective; just as entrepreneurial motives might serve the public interest, but that is not by design. LBO-led takeovers in the 1980s, for example, unquestionably shook up complacent and wasteful managements that had lost their competitive zeal. Instead of maximizing efficiency, too many firms had settled into a comfortable routine of peaceful coexistence. Under new LBO controllership, acquired companies took long-overdue steps to reduce costs, eliminate redundant layers of management. and sell off underperforming divisions or businesses.

On the negative side, it is apparent that some leveraged buyout practices are designed to show short-term results at the expense of long-term efficiency. Motivated to maximize cash flows in order to quickly reduce burdensome levels of debt assumed during a takeover, managements expediently slash capital expenditures, curtail research and development spending, and postpone maintenance, all actions that contradict sound management principles. In the end, the self-interest of controllers needs to be sorted out from those interests that serve the public welfare. When the rewards from promoting deals for companies far exceed those of managing the businesses themselves, it usually signals a need to reassess priorities. Just a glimpse of the super-rewards from one leveraged-buyout partnership suggests its fatal attraction.

> Between 1976 and 1982, KKR [Kohlberg Kravis Roberts] raised pools of money three times. The firm sank a total of $543 million into 20 different LBOs, including cupmaker Lily-Tulip and retailer Fred Meyer Inc. Most of the investments have been offloaded by now. On these completed deals. KKR realized profits of just over $1.5 billion. Compounded annual returns for investors in the three funds: 31%, 32% and 44%.[12]

Eventually, administrative managers resume command from controllers.[13] The latter have a limited interest and capability in the day-to-day chores of business management. That is not their primary skill, nor are they necessarily full-time managers while in control. Wall Street financial firms and entrepreneurial financiers do not seek "operational" responsibilities. Their view of companies is from an investor's point of view and it makes the controller's activities resemble those of a financier more than an industrialist.

Admittedly, this is an impressionistic picture of business dynamics that needs much detail work. Apart from Alfred Chandler, no author has probed deeply into the administrative and strategic interactions accompanying the rise of the large corporation in the United States. Nor have Chandler's landmark works been updated and expanded. Nor has there been any success in reconciling a historic view of business growth with modern notions of firm strategy and development.

Modern giant multi-business corporations literally have no theoretical basis for their existence. They have no past and no future, in a literary sense. Modern textbooks cannot furnish a connecting rationale that would explain present size and complexity based on their modest beginnings. If only conventional tactics of specialization were economically justifiable, or if industry sectors were rigid and unchanging, as is commonly assumed, the anatomy of big business would be much different than it is. In short, myth has replaced reality and theory has stayed aloof from the facts.

To return to realism, certain new assumptions would need to be woven into the fabric of theory: for example, big companies would be largely self-financing and would operate as entities separate from their shareholders, seeking both economies of scope and specialization, with administrative systems invented to handle strategic innovations, and with an integrated global view of competition. Such a multidimensional view of business is outside any frame of reference that currently exists.

Idealized explanations of firm behavior have so far been developed without the firm in the central role; this is rather similar to telling the story of Noah without the ark. An emphasis on markets has masked the rising influence of the major participants within markets. This focus on forests instead of trees creates the illusion of calm, even while frenetic internal movement is taking place. The uncertainty of change attributable to entrepreneurial activity is overlooked, as is the difference in strategies due to contrasts in managerial styles. Motivation of "controllers" versus "administrators," as just one example, leads to development of different maximizing strategies. Unless explicit account is taken of the motivations of those in charge of businesses, there is no basis for understanding the moves business makes or the appropriateness of business people's actions. Mechanistic models cannot explain deviations from their predicted outcomes, except to treat them as irrational or abnormal. A rigid formality accommodates only as many facts as fit. Generating hypotheses from the inside out, on the other hand, allows the investigator to scan externally in order to generate assumptions reasonably close to what actually occurs. Only after empirically testing and evaluating alternative hypotheses will consensus emerge on the most productive direction for future research.

Figure 3.1 suggests a framework that emphasizes a link between control and motivation (or strategy). Beginning with who is in control – whether a controller, an administrative manager, or secondary types under either category – helps to explain the rationality behind organizational activity.

When I wrote *Managing the Unmanageable*, I failed to appreciate fully the significance of this connection. Assuming organizational control would continue to be vested in professional managers, I extrapolated the movement into unrelated businesses by large, mature corporations, based on a

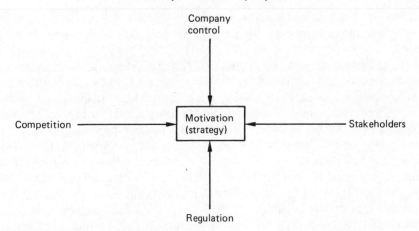

Figure 3.1 Framework for studying business change and progression

historic striving by managers for survival through growth. In the long run, the constancy of this underlying motivation should reassert itself. After every revolutionary epoch, administrators once again have assumed command. The destabilizing influence of rapid change, even if it is innovative and helpful in jogging companies free of inertia, takes time to assimilate and integrate into a cohesive organizational culture. No firm could perform effectively, if it were facing constant flux. Intervals of relative calm and bureaucratic administration always follow periods of major policy shifts.

But each generational age of administrators tends to differ from their predecessors. Administrators learn from experience. For example, seeing haphazardly assembled conglomerates as targets of financial restructuring in the 1980s has imposed a lesson, and a discipline, that will not be forgotten. The type of diversification seen in the 1950s and 1960s will not be repeated. Nevertheless, the urge to diversify will only be rechanneled, not stopped. The economies realizable from diversified size will replace the temporary hype to earnings from building gerrymandered enterprises lacking an operational justification.

In a movement already under way, diversified corporations are rationalizing the boundaries of a sustainable diversification strategy; they are staking out fewer areas in which to grow, where strong market positions can be acquired or built, and are divesting acquisitions or divisions that fall outside the strategic realm of management's vision of the type of company it wants to be. These are sensible moves, even displaying common sense. The outline for this style of diversification strategy was spelled out in *Managing the Unmanageable* and will be taken up once again in chapter 4 below. The message is basic: successful strategy in a single-business firm comprises a few basic concepts executed extremely well; for a multi-business firm, the concepts are different and take a significantly longer time to master.

In combination with the element of "control," factors of competition, stakeholders, and regulation are shown in figure 3.1. These are moderating influences on firm behavior. Using this framework for analysis, the "what is" of a particular firm or industry can be constructed. From there, "what should be" can be ventured. Without the interim step, suggestions for improving or reforming businesses seldom make a convincing case. For over half a century, the decisions of chief executives to diversify into different industries could only be explained as irrational when examined within the context of a methodology that saw excellence solely through the narrow lens of specialization. Researchers construed the tactics of hundreds of business firms over several decades in light of their own set of values and found business to be wanting. Within the fixed limits of a perfect model, there can be no allowance for results not consistent with the model's assumptions. Consequently, the alternatives have been either to ignore management's actions or to view them as illogical. When a new strategy of diversification took hold in the 1960s, there was no formal means to counter what conceptually could only be seen as an inefficient and ruinous way to run a business. Ideology took over, as the following quotation illustrates.

> When faced with a truly dangerous phenomenon, such as the conglomerate mergers of the 1960's, produced by financial manipulation making grist for their security mills, the professional antitrust economists were silent. Like other realities of a modern enterprise, this phenomenon, *which will probably subvert management effectiveness and organizational rationale for generations*, is outside their conceptual framework.[14]

Even today, unrelated diversification is seen as an aberrant phenomenon. Instead of relying on field studies to check on the accuracy of theory, the process is reversed.

Figure 3.1 is an attempt to return to the first principle of scientific research: the establishment of the facts. If one assumes that traditional administrative managers determine organizational strategy, then survival and growth will be key motivating forces behind firm development, pursuant to the lessons from more than 150 years of modern business history. Further, external pressures will keep managers from acting completely independently or arbitrarily. Figure 3.1 includes three major external factors: competition, stakeholders, and regulation. Each factor has played a significant part in shaping the way organizations have developed. And each major factor may encompass a number of specific topics that fit within it. For example, global competition is a possible subheading under "competition" that is a critical dimension for large multinational corporations, and thus warrants particular attention.

Seen from a top-level perspective, the exercise becomes one of predicting the forces that are driving a firm, an industry, or the general economy. The objective of such a framework is not to give precise answers, but to allow for a variety of questions to be tailored to the needs of different users. Its design can function as a tool serving a range of applications, from governmental policy to business decision-making. It is purposefully flexible in order to avoid a single-purpose, one-time point of view. As an illustration, each key factor is discussed below from the vantage point of national policy, supposing an evaluation was desired of the global competitiveness of American industry or for the appropriateness of current domestic antitrust policy.

Competition

Until comparatively recently, the USA was a dominant global economic presence, powerful abroad and without major pressures from foreign competition it its home markets. This has changed drastically and rapidly. In the near future, US firms could be waging a battle for control of global markets, hampered by entry rules favoring foreign competitors whose markets are less open than those of the USA.

In this day and age, a globally potent organization requires a transnational strategy. Companies must be able to produce from within major industrialized markets in order to avoid tariff and other restrictions placed on imports. Frequently, the quickest and most feasible means to achieve significant penetration in foreign markets is through acquisitions – a point not lost on the major trading partners of the USA.

British companies have led the list of foreign acquirers of American firms, with the West Germans in close pursuit. The Japanese have yet to stalk US companies aggressively, but this is a matter of timing and customary caution in Japanese decision-making, which cannot be counted on to prevail indefinitely. For Japan to participate in some of America's largest and most attractive industries, like food and pharmaceuticals, for example, it must depart from a traditional reliance on exports. And since representation in the American market is the key to becoming a world player, acquisitions will probably play a greater future role as Japan seeks to increase its presence in selected US markets. Indeed, Japan has already made strides toward becoming a world player in mergers and acquisitions (see table 3.3). In the first seven months of 1988, Japanese firms bought 95 companies worth $9 billion, according to the Industrial Bank of Japan. That compares with 146 acquisitions in all of 1987, worth $6.4 billion,

Table 3.3 Major Japanese acquisitions in the USA in 1988

Investor company	Target company (parent)	Price ($m)
Bridgestone Corporation	Firestone Tire & Rubber	2.6
Seibu/Saison Group	Intercontinental Hotel (Grand Metropolitan PLC)	2.2
Nippon Mining	Gould	1.1
Paloma Industries	Rheem Mfg (Pace Industries)	0.85
California First Bank (Bank of Tokyo, Ltd)	Union Bank of California (Standard Chartered PLC)	0.75
Settsu	Uarco (Kohlberg Kravis Roberts)	0.55
Shiseido	Zotos International (Conair)	0.35
Jusco	Talbots (General Mills)	0.33
Ryobi Ltd	Motor Products (Singer)	0.33
Kao	Andrew Jergens (American Brands)	0.30

which in turn was double the figures of the previous year. A recent survey of Japanese companies showed that 67 percent were interested in making acquisitions; three years ago, the corresponding figure was 20 percent.[15]

As in its merchandise-trade experience with Japan, the USA will be ill prepared to contest equally with Japan in any bilateral merger and acquisition exchange. Cultural and policy barriers impede the acquisition of Japanese companies, whereas a relatively open market allows Japanese corporations to buy American companies.

In general, US companies face many more barriers in buying foreign companies than foreign firms face in making acquisitions in the United States. In Japan, an interlocking system of ownership arrangements, plus concentration of shares in banks and other institutions that would be hostile to foreign takeovers, precludes the same free-wheeling approach to changes in ownership that is characteristic of merger and acquisition activity in the USA.

In Britain, West Germany, Italy, and other European nations, a much more active role is taken by government in monitoring and approving acquisitions by foreign firms. In addition, the barriers against acquiring control are complex and often subtle. In West Germany, for example, companies may be practically, if not legally, out of play: West German firms "have the ultimate 'shock repellent.' Often, the shares that trade don't have voting rights; control of the company is held by a higher class of preferred shares. And the preferred share voting is usually controlled by a supervisory board of outsider directors and large shareholders."[16]

In a potentially heated world-wide market of transnational acquisitions, the USA would be further hampered by accounting rules that favor foreign bidders.[17] Finally, consolidation of the European Community into one Common Market scheduled for completion by 1992 will give those firms inside the Community an expanded power base in Europe from which to extend their global reach.

Long-accustomed to being the "biggest" in major international as well as domestic markets, the USA may witness a further diminution of its influence, as giant foreign multinational firms consolidate and concentrate transnationally.

Stakeholders

In a conventional portrayal of corporate governance, managers' and share-holders' interests are usually the only ones deemed worthy of study. This two-dimensional perspective has recently been broadened, so that it is now common to see references to "stakeholders" rather than just share-holders. Stung by the ease with which shareholders could be persuaded to surrender their votes, and thereby control of even the largest corporations, company managements have become involved in extending the frame of their reference beyond shareholders to include customers, employees, suppliers, government, and other external constituencies that have a stake in how a particular business is run as well as an influence in reshaping the thinking on how corporate governance should work. It is increasingly apparent that successful firms must not stop at formulating sound business strategies, but must also seek the support and commitment of a variety of "stakeholders" in order to carry them out.

One stakeholder group that is potentially influential is labor. Frustrated by the job and personal dislocations caused by corporate restructurings, employee groups have tried to wrest control for themselves. This tactic was attempted, but without success, in labor disputes between Allegis (the parent of United Airlines) and Eastern Airlines, where unions made attempts to buy control of the carrier from the parent. When Atlantic & Pacific, the large food company, planned to make drastic cuts in operations, an employee-led group saved the jobs of many unionized workers by buying a number of stores from A & P and creating a new supermarket chain.

A variation of employee ownership is to use employee retirement plans to purchase a large percentage of the firm's shares and thereby make takeover more difficult, if not impossible. McLouth Steel Products, for example, used an employee stock-ownership plan (ESOP) in a novel effort by the union, in cooperation with the management, the state of Michigan, and interested community groups, to save more than two thousand jobs.

None of these possibilities currently constitutes more than a shadow on the horizon. On the other hand, the "old" management–shareholder bond is already frayed. In some companies, management has tried to tip the balance of control more in its favor by making the firm private through a leveraged buyout thereby avoiding the uncertainties of public ownership altogether. Initially, management-led leveraged buyouts were devised as a defensive strategy: a last-ditch resort to escape an unfriendly advance from a company or an entrepreneur who threatened managers' jobs as well as dismemberment of the company. More recently, managers have sought the leveraged buyout as a proactive means for converting a public company into a private one, thus reaping directly the potential rewards of good management, while avoiding the whims of the shareholder group. Significantly, recombining ownership and control in working managers re-establishes a strong incentive for managers to optimize the efficiency of the firm, thereby eliminating the ever-present prospect for conflicts of interest when ownership and management rests in separate hands.

There are built-in limitations to how effectively the traditional management–shareholder system can work to further both the professional aims of managers and the financial goals of investors. New ways of combining ownership with control will conceivably emerge and promote better overall efficiency than perpetuation of the structure that is in place.

Regulation

A third factor both policy-makers and business managers must consider is the climate and timing for new rules and regulations. Businesses are no less driven by self-interest than when Adam Smith wrote. It remains for a higher authority to establish the guidelines that allow maximum individual freedom, while protecting the collective interests of society as a whole.

In the 1960s, when the conglomerate frenzy was in full swing, part of the stimulus was due to overliberal accounting and tax treatment that were allowed when two businesses were combined. New rules governing such accounting and tax incentives lessened the frenzied pace and speculation that was inherent in the conglomerate movement. In similar fashion, reforms have been prompted that address certain undesirable aspects of corporate restructuring in the 1980s. The Tax Reform Act of 1986, for example, contained a technical provision abolishing "mirrors" – a loophole allowing the buying and selling of companies without payment of a capital gains tax. Also, several states passed legislation in the 1980s that was intended to diminish the adverse impact of takeovers on companies in their territorial jurisdiction. Congress further considered restrictive rules on "golden parachutes" – a device whereby company executives receive generous "bail-out" compensation packages, if their firm is acquired and/ or they leave the company as a result of a takeover. These are unlikely to be the final acts of response by regulators, if the heated activity in restructuring starts to boil over.

Attempts at legislative reform generally do not stop mergers and acquisitions from happening. At most, they moderate a movement's tempo and longevity. New rules are sometimes needed in order to remove undesirable incentives for speculation in company shares, while at the same time keeping markets relatively free so that new business combinations can be formed that raise overall industry efficiency. Without such a balance, the three movements toward consolidation, conglomeration, and restructuring in this century would all have tended toward greater speculative excess.

In the present environment, restructuring activity seems destined for more "corrective" legislation, while retaining its legitimacy as a permanent instrument of corporate strategy. Indeed, assuming continued acquiescence by the Justice Department's antitrust division, and the relaxed attitude toward bigness by academic experts, more national and international acquisitions and divestitures seem assured. The more important concern now is to see that rules are uniformly applied, avoiding a tilt toward particular individuals, firms, industries, or countries, in order to assure that the participants with the best economic case for building more efficient organizations are the winners.

Differentiation Among Strategic Business Groups

The issues managements choose to address are all-important. Given the right focus, a number of alternative strategies can generally get a company from here to there. With top management's attention riveted in the right direction, the margin of error can be significant and still produce results superior to systematic analysis of matters with little import.

Figure 3.1 attempts to capture the essence of directional problem-solving. The specifics of the design are not the critical element; different factors might be substituted and still retain the validity of the concept. The framework of figure 3.1 provides a focus for decision-making. It is intended as an idea generator. Models do not make decisions; people do. Once the decision has been made to study an issue, the individual settings, resources, and personalities of companies will dictate the specifics of the solutions that emerge.

Figure 3.1 offers a simple, but flexible tool that can be used in a vast array of applications. The sparse construction of figure 3.1 is given substance by differentiating along a number of dimensions. For example, it is extremely unlikely that firms with few common denominators can be usefully served by a single all-encompassing model. Conversely, looking at relatively small groups of companies with shared characteristics can illuminate the natural attributes that "strategic groups" have in common. Strategy formulation in big businesses, for example, takes account of different factors than in small firms. Mature companies differ from emerging companies.

Technology firms contrast with commodity-type businesses. Multinational corporations do not face the same problems as domestic firms. Differentiating by types of managers, levels of diversification, life-cycle stages, and by industries offers potentially sharper insights than treating "business" as a homogeneous entity with one mind and a single purpose.

The premise for figure 3.1 is a belief that a combination of simplicity and differentiation works more effectively than a complex theory equally confining for all companies and every contingency. Attempts to shoehorn every configuration of business into the same mold risks missing the essential differences on which corporate strategy depends. Moreover, research is forced into a repetitive and narrow line of investigation. The underlying presumption is that companies are essentially the same, yet the very purpose of strategy is to comprehend how superior management can make a difference.

Furthermore, frameworks of analysis that recognize differences among "strategic groups" of companies also permit greater focus on uniformities *within* such groups. Only by grouping companies that have much in common can regularities reasonably be expected to be uncovered. The more closely companies resemble one another, either through strategy or structure or major organizational traits, the more unified their group actions would tend to be. Within these common contexts, the precision and power of science could be brought to bear most fruitfully, and revealingly. For the multi-faceted business scene, looking for small "pockets" of uniformity promises a greater payoff than a single monolithic survey.

Perversely, as the world grows more complex, science-based models of business tend to get simpler. Rationality in decision-making grows stronger as uncertainty increases. This upside-down view of the world reflects badly on the supposed objectivity of management scholarship. By definition, the study of firms is a micro-level phenomenon. Only by investigating individual firms, in uncertain and changing industry states, can the competitive realities facing actual managers be grasped. Where different philosophies and motivations prevail, they should be recognized. When companies differ, and when they act in concert, should be what determines the method of analysis that is appropriate. As John Neville Keynes wisely observed "according to the special department or aspect of the science under investigation, the appropriate method may be either abstract or realistic, deductive or inductive, mathematical or statistical, hypothetical or historical."[18]

Applying the Lessons of Experience

Let us keep a rigorously scientific demeanor as an integral part of management studies, by all means. It is a methodology preferable to all others in the study of regularities and recurring patterns. Where it applies, use it. Where it does not, do not force it. The practice of business is by nature an imperfect process. Not only is the level of complexity enormous, but the need to filter a multiplicity of factors through the "bounded rationality" of human decision-makers adds to the uncertainty. Overlaying "perfect" models onto an imperfect world gives precisely wrong answers.

A new course in "Business Policy" was recommended in the Ford and Carnegie sponsored studies on higher education in business. It was proposed that this course would deal specifically with the ambiguity of decision-making at the top, with case work suggested as the principal teaching tool to capture the open-ended and individualistic nature of actual business problems. By substituting artificially "perfect" models of business as the focus of study, this original purpose is compromised. More than that, the profession risks intellectual prejudice against "realistic" scholarship.

Economists in particular are insular and communal in attitude, fiercely resisting any enlightenment from outside their "private" world. As a now famous economist recalls, the profession strongly discouraged his initiatives beyond the accepted limits of orthodoxy. Specifically, his mentors at the University of Chicago resisted his efforts at integrating a global perspective into his work:

> In all my training at Chicago there was no serious mention of the global system. Chicago training, like training elsewhere, was closed economic training . . . So I did the only thing I could: I jettisoned Chicago economics. But that left me in an intellectual vacuum . . . I was intellectually exposed. I disassociated myself from a whole set of personal friendships developed over a 20-year period. Every time I made a move I was accused of inconsistency or disloyalty. I was frozen out of the "money river." I felt like a pariah.[19]

Unfortunately, the same type of tunnel vision still prevails in economics. Matters of policy cannot be handled, given the inflexible methods of the profession. This prevents some of the best and brightest minds in the country from addressing the very serious problems and uncertainties facing American industry. Each of the major factors in figure 3.1, for example, deserves greater scrutiny than it is receiving. There are enough promising areas of research to keep many future generations of investigators productively occupied. Instead, the same sterile theories get chewed into smaller and smaller pieces, producing personal rewards within the academic system, but almost a dead loss from the standpoint of business and the nation.

Business studies cannot avoid a policy orientation. Its mandate is to develop the strategies and structures that can be applied to solve practical business problems. The science of management occupies only a fraction of that space. By embracing the certainties of scientific methods, business studies turns away from the side of business that gives it special relevance and meaning to the business community.

Summary

Managers live with uncertainty every day. Strategic, forward-looking, and irreversible decisions are not wholly susceptible to formal methods of analysis. Corporate-level strategy that determines what position a firm takes within an industry or in different industries is the most uncertain and strategic decision that managers must make. If the job of management scholars is to help business managers perform more effectively, then a trade-off between science and art is necessary. Techniques must be designed for the level of complexity encountered.

The "what is" of business taught in classrooms and contained in textbooks is not validated by history. Neither revolutionary nor normal evolutionary progress can be adequately explained by reference to any of the principal frameworks in use. In none of these is the firm the focal point, nor is motivation of those who manage a key element. Without this orientation, it is impossible to reconcile the current status of business with its beginnings.

Prevailing theories make no distinction between the entrepreneur and the traditional administrative manager. Dynamic reconstruction of business through innovative strategies – a Schumpeterian scenario – lies outside the highly idealized concepts of firm behavior. And diversification of firms away from a core business is viewed as theoretically flawed, even though business managements act differently.

The reasons for denying what may be observed directly are concerned with methodology. By taking a positivistic approach, only so much realism can be accommodated. As business changes, the element of realism diminishes. Having chosen an inflexible model, an internal consistency must be maintained in order to preserve the model's integrity. Two of the most enduring "myths" created for this purpose are assumptions of "firm specialization" and "industry stability." With these conceptually limiting dimensions, moves by business managers are circumscribed. For example, strategy is reduced to a business-level proposition, since specialization is the only "justifiable" strategy. Industry diversification, as a corporate-level strategy, does not fit the assumptions.

A precise and inflexible methodology can deal only partially, at best, with the organic, changing, uncertain, and progressive nature of business. The idea of figure 3.1 is to focus on 'what is" in business through an open-ended framework that acknowledges the uncertain and changeable aspects of managerial work. In contrast to a closed system, the answers forthcoming are likely to vary considerably. This does not mean that no useful generalizations can be developed. To the contrary, the level of usefulness can be significantly raised by tailoring such a framework to a number of "strategic groupings" of businesses. Within each group, commonalities can suggest similar types of strategies to be followed. Compartmentalizing businesses along common lines simultaneously complicates and simplifies the study of business. Just as in real life, there is no master key that opens every door or solves every problem. It is a painstaking process of investigation that is made no less difficult by assuming the complexities away.

Notes

1 John Neville Keynes, *The Scope and Method of Political Economy* (Macmillan, New York, 1897), p. 35.
2 Ibid., p. 28.
3 Michael C. Jenson and William H. Meckling, "Theory of the firm: managerial behavior, agency costs and ownership structure," *Journal of Financial Economics*, 3 (1976), p. 311. Two other reviews of "agency theory" are Roger Clarke and Tony McGuiness, *The Economics of the Firm* (Basil Blackwell, Oxford, 1987); and John W. Pratt and Richard J. Zeckhauser, *Principals and Agents: The Structure of Business* (Harvard Business School Press, Boston, Mass., 1985).
4 C. Joseph Pusateri, *A History of American Business* (Harlon Davidson, Arlington Heights, Ill., 1984), p. 200.
5 Jonathan Hughes, *The Vital Few*, expanded edn (Oxford University Press, Oxford, 1986), p. 424.
6 *Fortune*, 29 February 1988, p. 44.
7 J. S. Mill gloomily forecast in 1848 that "the theory of value was complete. In a generation the theory he had in mind was utterly displaced," in Robert Lekachman, *The Age of Keynes* (Vintage Books, New York, 1966), p. 67. As late as this decade, the popular misconception of stability stubbornly persists: "By 1915, the American business scene had assumed much the same shape which it retains today," in Pusateri, *A History of American Business*, p. 177.
8 M. Casson, *The Entrepreneur: An Economic Theory* (Barnes & Nobel, Totowa, NJ, 1982), p. 9.
9 *Wall Street Journal*, 3 May 1988, p. 30.
10 Steady-state and evolutionary, with the approximate meanings of evolutionary and revolutionary, were used previously by Milton Leontiades, *Strategies for Diversification and Change* (Little, Brown, Boston, Mass., 1980), esp. p. 73.
11 *Fortune*, 19 February 1988, p. 50.
12 Ibid., p. 47.
13 See Hughes, *The Vital Few*, p. 11; also Alfred D. Chandler, Jr and Herman Daems, eds, *Managerial Hierarchies* (Harvard University Press, Cambridge, Mass., 1980), p. 13.

14 Robert Solo, "New maths and old sterilities," *Saturday Review*, 22 January 1972, p. 47. (My italics.)
15 *Wall Street Journal*, 10 November 1988, p. A18.
16 *Wall Street Journal*, 22 March 1988, p. 7.
17 *Wall Street Journal*, 24 March 1988, p. 30.
18 Keynes, *The Scope and Method of Political Economy*, p. 30.
19 Leonard A. Rapping, in Arjo Klamer, *Conversations with Economists*, (Rowman and Allanheld, New Jersey, 1983), p. 227.

4
Diversification for Better Performance

A major part of the book so far has been devoted to exposing management myths, because what is perceived to be true can be as critical as the truth itself. Where cause-and-effect relationships are unclear, the propositions that gain currency rely, to a large degree, on a strong defense. Persons who question the current orthodoxy must first contend with the defenses surrounding it. Part of the defensive shield surrounding the so-called theory of the firm is the rules established by the defenders: in particular, the rule that only a "more perfect" theory can displace an existing one. Although detractors may point to observable inconsistencies of current theory, such criticisms go unheeded unless a more elegant explanation can be offered in substitution. Since we live in an imperfect world, this puts a premium on being exact rather than being right. Not feeling bound by these rules frees one to explore an opposite, and more enlightening, proposition: a factual basis for the development of a practical understanding of firm behavior and, specifically, the diversification strategy of firms.

In this chapter, the emphasis shifts from "what is not," in terms of the conduct of business, to a positive presentation of some of the things that are believed to be factually accurate, even if they are not scientifically verifiable, as regards corporate diversification. The focus is on nonspecialized diversification: that is, deliberate moves by companies to diversify away from a core activity, generally through acquisitions of other firms with minimal operational linkages to the acquirer. The investigation of such a strategy of nonspecialized diversification is looked at along three dimensions:

1 the sense of nonspecialized diversification;
2 the strategy of nonspecialized diversification;
3 suggestions for improved results from nonspecialized diversification.

The Sense of Nonspecialized Diversification

The sense of any diversification strategy starts with the perspective of those who govern. Subject to external constraints, management chooses from a number of possible strategic options those best-suited to meet the company's objectives. The framework in figure 3.1 began with motivation and control for this reason. Without understanding the motives of those who control, there can be no mapping of where a firm will, or should, go.

Operations-minded managers – as opposed to financial controllers – have repeatedly expressed a desire for growth as the best means to assure survival. Once a company ceases to grow, it begins to decline. Other companies seeking to ascend the next rung toward the top keep the pressure on the firms above them to keep moving forward or fall behind.

When the race for bigness started, there was more than enough growth to keep available resources employed. Building enough capacity to satisfy demand was the main concern. And as long as demand remained strong, a firm could grow and prosper by following a simple one-product strategy. Nearly every big company started small and with a single major product. By plowing earnings back into the business, the big got bigger. By merging many competitors into one company, the biggest also got more powerful. To sustain growth, these large enterprises also acquired other companies, sustaining their growth by "feeding" on other firms and other processes in the same industry. To keep on growing, new technologies and new markets propelled firms into related businesses that capitalized on existing specialties or skills.

Growth by these means, however, eventually slows, as markets become saturated, and as mergers and acquisitions of competitors approach legal and practical limits. Product and market extensions seldom propel a firm with the same intensity as the original product innovation and virgin markets. As demand for old products recedes, and innovations fall short of taking up the slack, management is faced with a limiting set of alternatives: settle for slower growth, sell the firm, or give money back to shareholders in the form of higher dividends or through a buyback of shares. None of these options meets the primary drive to keep growing. The only other option consistent with a growth strategy is diversification, and if diversification into related businesses is blocked or unattractive, then the firm must diversify into new businesses.

Nonspecialized diversification, in sum, is the by-product of managerial motivations for growth in conjunction with competitive imperatives for survival. Given managers' "overriding concern for corporate survival,"[1] a turn away from specialization at some point is an understandable, if not predictable, strategy for firms to pursue. The life-cycle pattern traced out in corporate and industry histories of growth and evolution is a familiar theme in management literature.

Competitive pressures to excel, and a commitment to preserve the organization intact, are instinctive for American managers. The managerial system is geared toward rewarding ever higher revenues, and earnings, and the corporation is an embodiment of this system. An administrator's instinct pushes him to fulfilling the next logical step forward.

But is nonspecialized diversification good strategy? Just because managers seek to satisfy a natural instinct does not mean the results are beneficial for the firm or society at large. The national interest cannot be subordinated to the self-satisfaction of firm managers. In the long term, the strategies that managers pursue must further the building of competitive strength in individual firms and build a strong industrial capability nationwide.

Before attempting to measure the value of nonspecialized diversification, it is important to make the right kind of comparisons. A clear bias is introduced, for example, by indiscriminately comparing multi-business corporations against all other businesses. This is a common mistake in past statistical tests of performance; it mixes apples and oranges. Given a choice, and market conditions being the same, running a single business is clearly preferable to all other alternatives. The best business is the simplest, *everything else being equal*. It is only after market growth subsides that diversification is worth considering. The fallacy of drawing conclusions from contrasting companies in different industries and at different stages in their development cycle is made apparent in the following analogy:

> At the start of the 1970s any executive in full possession of his senses would have traded an Avon for a GE any day. Avon's elementally simple idea of door-to-door selling by agents yielded almost one third of GE's anxieties. Yet Avon's day was soon to be done. As its market worsened and its method became obsolescent, Avon slipped – until on a ninth of GE's sales it was earning only a twelfth of the giant's net.[2]

The proper basis for comparison, therefore, is between a nonspecialized company and a specialized company with the same core business, one company having chosen to diversify away from that core business, while the other company stayed specialized. For example, United States Steel could be compared with an Armco (steel); Sears with a J. C. Penney (mass merchandising); or General Electric with a Maytag (major appliances). Another possible line of investigation is to compare the fortunes of companies that have diversified with their probable outcomes had they remained in their original lines of business: would Textron be a better performer today, had it remained in the textile business, for example, or if

Gulf + Western had stuck with automotive parts, or Tenneco had remained a gas transmission company?

Definitive answers are hard to come by. Reconstruction of data to permit valid comparisons is next to impossible. Audit trails back through time are extremely difficult to retrace. Also, the contribution to revenues from acquired, as opposed to internal, growth would pose thorny problems of disaggregation. No classification scheme, or data-driven analysis, could completely resolve all the "what if" type of questions that could be raised. Whatever the technique, data alone cannot supply the answers: "If you go to the data thinking that mergers on average have zero net social effect, you come away from the data with the same thought."[3]

Reliance on empirical analyses alone can never reveal the proper role and contribution of acquisitions to firm strategy. Efforts to date in this direction have yielded poor results. Belatedly, a glimmer of acknowledgement – but little more – has made its way into the scholarly literature admitting a need for further conceptual development to enhance our understanding of diversity and performance.[4]

In developing a better insight, comments from practitioners are worth heeding. The most influential reasons, after all, are those that are persuasive to managers who make actual decisions. Harold Geneen, who was responsible for creating the conglomerate called ITT, put forward the following list of seven reasons that attracted him to one or another of the many nonspecialized acquisitions that ITT made during his reign as its top executive.[5]

1 To diversify into industries and markets that have good prospects for above-average long-term growth and profitability.
2 To achieve a sound balance between foreign earnings and domestic earnings.
3 To achieve a sound balance between high-risk capital-intensive manufacturing operations and less risky service operations.
4 To achieve a sound balance between high-risk engineering-labor-intensive electronics manufacturing and less risky commercial and industrial manufacturing.
5 To achieve a sound ratio between commercial/industrial products and services, and consumer products and services.
6 To achieve a sound ratio between government/defense/space operations, and commercial/industrial/consumer products and services in both foreign and domestic markets.
7 To achieve a sound balance between cyclical products and services.

The items above describe the "motives and purposes" for ITT's acquisitions and apply generally to other firms as well. Similarly, the grounds on which Geneen justified the acquisitions made by ITT – "to provide growth, and security for our employees and stockholders" – echo present-day sentiments. The mere itemization of these reasons, however, does not make a summary case for accepting diversification as superior to specialization.

Framing Geneen's comments in a broader context, the basic point at issue is whether administration of companies within a "family of businesses" offers advantages that the "single business" does not. Coordinating activities within firms versus through markets implicitly has *some* merit, or else businesses – even single businesses – would not have incorporated in the first place. An extension of this logic is to ask whether a "family of businesses" affords a comparative advantage in certain circumstances that is not conferred on single businesses operating on their own.

Deciding on extending the administrative reach of firms into new industries rests entirely on the efficacy with which resources can be managed. Efficiency serves as the basic criterion to prefer administered transactions over market contracting in any context. Therefore, nonspecialization must be justified over specialization based on gains in relative efficiency. It remains to be shown, in other words, if broadening the scope of activities under a single administrative structure results in a net benefit. By absorbing more than one specialty, can corporations raise the efficiency of combined operations to more than offset inefficiencies from trying to manage and control a less unified organization? Let us examine the positive potential from nonspecialized diversification first.

Firm Efficiencies Created by Diversification

1 Advantages of size plus scope   Whereas diversification is *possible* by relying on specialization as the principal strategy, the limits of specialization impose constraints and contrast with the objective of nonspecialized diversification. A company seeking to diversify, but remain specialized looks for opportunities to build "connections" between itself and the companies it acquires. Using Michael Porter's value-chain concept, it attempts to connect itself to its acquired units at as many parts of the value chain as possible. The more sharing of activities or resources between a parent company and its various parts, the better. This implies that a company should only diversify into related businesses, with which it can share either production facilities, distribution channels, sales forces, or other common elements. This places the premium on *remaining specialized*, with nonspecialized diversification only applicable in those exceptional situations where link-ups are possible.

Nonspecialized diversification, on the other hand, makes entry into new markets its principal objective. Companies deliberately distance themselves from old businesses in order to escape the confines of operating in a single industry. This de-emphasizes the importance of connectedness. As a result, specialized diversifiers stay close to what they know, whereas nonspecialized diversifiers eschew too close a relationship with their past.

Consequently, synergy is possible from either a specialized or a nonspecialized approach to diversification, but it is of a different kind. For one thing, companies operating in different industries do not share specialized skills at the business level. There are, however, some opportunities for specialty-sharing at the corporate level. For example, two common types of specialty-sharing within a family of different businesses occur in the areas of planning and financial controls. In each of these functions, acquired businesses avoid the start-up expenses and expertise assumed by the parent. In planning, for example, the skills of a multi-business parent generally exceed those of a firm concentrated in but one industry. By necessity, a widely diversified company has invested in the development of a planning system to control its complex organization. This learning experience benefits the individual businesses it acquires, since these inherit a sophisticated method for strategic planning that they have neither the talent, resources, nor incentive to develop on their own.

Financial controls represent a similar opportunity for the sharing of centralized expertise. Upon acquiring a business, a parent imposes a system of accountability that assures a minimum level of financial competency. Moreover, the post-acquisition audit – a basic part of the acquisition process – may help uncover and rectify ways of doing business that have outlived their original rationale, if one ever existed. When cost accounting was first introduced at Ford Motor Company, for example, it was discovered that the company was losing \$62 on every car.[6] More recently, when Lee Iaccoca took over as chief executive officer at Chrysler, he was amazed at the lack of financial controls: "I couldn't find out anything," he exclaimed, "This was probably the greatest jolt I've ever had in my business career."[7] Independent and objective appraisals, like those at Ford and Chrysler, resemble in principle the audits conducted as part of post-acquisition procedures.

Opportunities may also exist for the pooling of research and development resources, where common interests exist, even if individual businesses operate in fundamentally different markets. Honeywell, for instance, has proclaimed electronic control systems to be an element connecting its wide-ranging mix of revenues from heating thermostats, automation systems, avionics equipment, and sophisticated torpedoes. By combining resources to pursue advanced research in "electronic controls"– in addition to specialized research at the business level – Honeywell can build a capability that its businesses could not hope to match.

Scope offers an added advantage in the hiring, retention, and promotion of managers. Within a single business, the hierarchy is well defined and difficult to catapult. Only so many slots are open at any one time and even well-qualified managers take a place in the queue. A diversified company, on the other hand, has a broader placement set to offer current and prospective employees, thereby reducing the chances of immobilizing and losing talented workers.

Finally, an exceptionally well-managed diversified company can uplift the performance of firms it acquires in a variety of nonquantifiable dimensions: for example, higher *esprit*, better culture, stronger ethics, tighter quality standards, or more positive motivation. General Electric, for instance, has always been a pacesetter in business planning, organizational design, financial controls, and technology. Although a conglomerate, General Electric actively monitors the progress of each business; it ensures that each unit measures up to the parent's high standards. Superior management in a number of areas is a hard-won achievement that gives General Electric a real, although intangible, asset that it uses to raise the basic skills of the companies it acquires.

A well-managed nonspecialized diversifier like General Electric need not sacrifice advantages of large scale. Diversification to achieve a wider scope of operations incorporates advantages of size, but goes beyond them. A large diversified company can potentially achieve the same economies of scale *in each business* as a large specialized company.

If all firms were equally well managed, the principal economies from diversification would be those of scale and only intra-industry mergers would make sense. But if management skills are less than perfectly distributed *among* industries, it would be anti-competitive to prevent better-managed companies from seeking out underperformers, wherever they might be. It would be unusual indeed if superbly managed companies in one industry could impart nothing of value into industries other than their own. The ultimate payoff, of course, depends on successfully implementing the strategy of nonspecialized diversification. However, to uphold as a basic law of management that nonspecialized diversification contains no economic rationale seems itself implausible.

2 Improved financial efficiency Once a firm is part of a corporate family, there are certain undeniable benefits from associating with a financially stronger parent. Cost of capital, for one, tends to be lower when borrowings are backed by the parent's superior credit rating. Businesses that are growing very rapidly generally cannot generate enough funds through operations to satisfy their investment needs, and the cumulative-cost savings from using less costly capital can be considerable. These types of businesses – paired with a mature parent company that generates excess cash – balance cash sources and uses in a way that benefits both acquirer and acquiree.

Avoiding the uncertainty of relying on financial conditions in the capital market, a parent corporation can systematically plan for, and reserve, the amount of future funding needed by its divisions. Moreover, the corporation can ensure the availability of funding on demand. Having evaluated the payoff from investment in a particular business, headquarters will make sure that the business does not fail for lack of enthusiasm by outside investors. There is sharing of information and confidences that is impossible to duplicate in an impersonal marketplace. Also, the parent organization is better positioned to judge the level of risks entailed by one of its units for a particular investment. Within the corporation, in short, every member enjoys preferred treatment. Other things being equal, financial backing stands out as a clear positive factor from nonspecialized diversification.[8]

If capital markets were perfectly efficient and informed in arriving at investment decisions, the financial rewards from forming a "family of businesses" would be diminished. Here, again, perceptions are all important. What managers believe to be true about efficiency is, in fact, what governs actions, whether or not they appear justified in an idealized setting. And according to business people's decisions, and from surveys of business person's opinions, managers consciously try to remove themselves from the discipline of the capital market.[9]

Part of the reason can undoubtedly be traced back to differences in judgment between markets and managers. Where possible, managers instinctively prefer to control the basis for making critical investments, rather than subject themselves to the whims of investors. As reflected by the opinions of corporate decision-makers, managers have learned from experience that "the only truly loyal money was money over which they had direct control."[10]

3   *Efficiency of resource allocation*   If managements have only one business to look after, that business will assuredly get all the attention and all the money. In a growing market, that is as it should be. When demand declines, however, the best decision of all may be to withhold investing in a low-growth business altogether. Given management's proclivity to grow, this is a hard conclusion to reach. In steel, for example, almost every "expert" study has pessimistically concluded that the once-dominant American steel industry will continue its relative decline. Yet investment decisions, as seen from management's eyes, are not so sanguinely evaluated. In companies where steel is the only business, it is the most irresistible of all investment alternatives.

Armco, a large steel company, ventured tentatively into insurance and financial services before hastily retreating back into steel. The exigencies of managing businesses they did not understand convinced Armco's management that the company was better off in steel. Almost all of Armco's top management team had backgrounds in metallurgical engineering, and although metallurgical engineers might know something about the metal business, the chief executive officer of Armco ventured that they "didn't understand the pitfalls" in insurance and financial services.[11] Thus Armco executives rejected diversification and retreated back into the safe harbour of a business they knew best. Consequently, the earnings retained in the business by Armco will go back into steel, even though, by the company's own actions, it is not an industry with a promising long-term future.

United States Steel stands unique among steel companies in aggressively moving into a major new activity by acquiring Marathon Oil and Texas Oil and Gas. Now United States Steel balances substantial revenues from energy against those from steel. By diversifying away from its core business, United States Steel opened a new channel for investing cash flows and reduced the risks of a sole dependency on steel. In the future, United States Steel vows to invest cash flows to further its strategy of diversifying from steel. However United States Steel's decision turns out, it is one management felt it had to make. Assuming the long-range prospects for integrated steel producers in the United States continue downward, other large domestic steel companies will have postponed, but not avoided, the hazards of staying with a specialty whose peak has long passed.

Demand in many basic industries is too low to employ all the world's capacity profitably. In addition to steel, glaring imbalances are prominent in automobiles, heavy equipment, and textiles, among others. Moreover, conditions promise to get worse before they get better, as country after country builds world-scale facilities.[12] Every large company clearly cannot profitably maintain an ever-growing scale of operations in industries that are already overburdened with excess capacity. Voluntarily, or through mergers or liquidations, excess capacity needs to shrink. The conditions for "creative destruction," à la Schumpeter, already exist. Only the means for correcting the supply imbalances remains to be worked out.

In a family of different businesses, objective decisions to quit, liquidate, or shrink capacity are easier to reach than in a single business. For one-industry firms, these decisions are tantamount to corporate suicide or dismemberment: an unnatural act, in corporations as well as humans. Whatever diminishes the firm's stature also reduces the source of management's own power and status. To expect managements to make detached decisions in such circumstances is naive. Managements normally hold survival of the firm as a paramount goal. During hardship, the instinct for survival strengthens. It is one thing to be objective when only quantifiable criteria feature in the decision; it is quite another matter when very personal considerations, like loss of job, affect the evaluation process.

Markets most often have been powerless to enforce competitiveness on managements that are determined to avoid facing hard realities. Only in exceptional cases have investors intervened to gain control of a corporation and steer it in a new direction. Given a choice, however, investors will typically seek control of mismanaged companies in growing industries rather than those in declining or slow-growth businesses. The aging process carries inevitable consequences that even superior management cannot change. Nor is downsizing or liquidation an easy decision to reach in a one-industry firm. In that circumstance, nonspecialized diversification becomes the alternative most consistent with management's philosophy of growth and survival.

What central management in a nonspecialized company provides is a discipline that the market often cannot give. Nonspecialized diversification combines management's inside knowledge of businesses under its control with the objective perspective of an investor who is not committed solely to any one investment. Because the diversified company has more than one outlet for its capital, it can dispassionately select where to commit resources, or cut back, based on greatest potential returns on capital. In the long run, this creates stronger competitors and enhances the level of economic efficiency generally.

Pratt and Whitney, a part of United Technologies and a leading manufacturer of aircraft engines, recently lost its top position to General Electric. Anxious to recoup, United Technologies is pouring money into its aircraft engine business. With its diversified base of operations, United Technologies is capable of putting considerable financial strength behind this concentrated effort. Had Pratt and Whitney been United Technologies's only business, it would have been difficult to recoup and reinvest on a scale necessary to challenge General Electric and regain its leadership spot.

Philip Morris and RJR-Nabisco, the top manufacturers of tobacco, faced a different type of challenge. Envisaging certain decline in domestic unit sales of cigarettes, both managements diversified into food-related businesses in a major way. In a relatively short time, for example, Philip Morris acquired General Foods and Kraft, two giant companies in different parts of the food business. These acquisitions provided Philip Morris with an alternative investment outlet for its huge excess cash flows from the tobacco business, plus an avenue for future growth and survival.

Finally, diversification does not ensure good decision-making, but it gives management the latitude to overcome miscalculations and unforeseeable contingencies. Every manager makes mistakes, and change is endemic to business. In a one-industry company, the consequences of staying specialized can prove disastrous for reasons beyond management's control, as in the case of the cigarette business, or for normal shifts in business fortunes, as in United Technologies' Pratt and Whitney division.

Relatively recently, General Motors sought to curtail automobile production capacity, while diversifying into nonautomotive businesses: "In the mid-1980s, at the time of the EDS and Hughes acquisitions, talk was about non-auto operations contributing 10% of GM's total revenues by 1990. Last year, they hit 12%. GM last year earned $10.06 a share, $6.68 of which came from activities only tangentially related to building cars."[13]

Had GM diversified earlier, perhaps it would have handled the Japanese invasion of its basic automobile business differently. As it was, there was little choice, but to react. Had GM not been so big and able to afford mistakes, and had not the US government established import quotas, the domestic automobile industry would undoubtedly have been restructured differently. And if GM had the "discipline" of an internal market of business choices, each seeking capital to grow, it may not have poured so much money into redundant facilities. In 1986 alone, in a series of unprecedented decisions, GM closed eleven plants. Clearly, the presumed "discipline" of market forces had not worked effectively in curbing such gross errors of judgment.

A free market, despite its considerable virtues, cannot discipline corporations that are beyond its reach. For mature businesses enjoying excess cash flows, the capital market can be largely avoided. Coupled with a declining demand curve, such mature businesses must either come under independent review of another sort or let the self-interest of management prevail, to the detriment of economic efficiency. In these cases, only the multi-business firm exerts a discipline similar to that of the capital market, because only in such an organization does one find – albeit in miniature – the multiplicity of investment options that is the hallmark of a competitive marketplace.

4 International efficiency   How do specialized companies in the United States combat nonspecialized foreign competitors? They fare poorly, in too many cases. America's most formidable competitors, the Japanese, seem unconcerned about whatever "danger" a nonspecialized philosophy portends. With the largest army of giant, conglomerate-style firms, the Japanese have methodically disproved the myth of specialization in one industry after another.

Protected only by an ingrained belief that conglomerates "should not work", the United States economy may be poorly positioned to counter the might of Japanese conglomerates that apparently do work. Another belated acknowledgement of short-sighted management by United States firms – if such proves to be the case – will come too late to save many companies in industries targeted for fierce foreign competition, with the consequence that many smaller and weaker firms will fall by the wayside.

Semiconductors is one such industry. Plagued by world-wide over-capacity – due to fast growth and overbuilding, rather than a drop in demand, in this instance – semiconductor manufacturers have already restructured and downsized. Small, innovative companies that used to set leading-edge technology now are focused on market niches using older technology. With costs soaring just to stay competitive, it is small wonder. Intel estimated that in 1986 it spent $100 million to develop its 80386 microprocessor chip. This doubled the amount of spending on the previous generation's chip, with the cost of designing the next generation likely to double again. From 1986 to the end of the decade, world-wide spending by the semiconductor industry should double from the previous four years, to about $50 billion on plant and equipment, plus an added $25 billion on research and development, according to one authority. Just to afford the massive research and development expenditures needed to remain a world player requires yearly sales of at least $1 billion. With this sharp increase in costs, more than half of the world's 300 chipmakers will disappear in the next decade, predicts Pasquale Pistorio, chief executive of SGS, the state-controlled Italian semiconductor manufacturer, who negotiated a merger with a subsidiary of Thomson, the large nationalized French electronics company, in order to assure SGS's survival in this world contest.[14]

However, size alone may not be enough. Size is an enabling strategy currently, but if competitors combine scope with scale, they may outmaneuver those who are merely big. General Electric's acquisition of RCA contains the potential of a combined strategy. By buying RCA, GE added two major business segments – RCA's defense work and NBC, the broadcast system – that are protected from foreign competition. This will add to GE's staying power against foreign competitors who have a number of pockets from which to push "targeted" areas of future growth. "Every day we're meeting the Toshibas of the world, the Hitachis of the world," says John F. Welch, Jr, chairman of GE. "We have to get larger and more powerful to be able to compete or just give up and let imports take over."[15]

Japan's policy of "targeting" key industries is well known. Carried out in textiles, shipbuilding, and petrochemicals, the strategic play is now being enacted in semiconductors. Offered inducements by the Japanese government, including some concessionary financing, and given the protection of their home market, where manufacturers buy Japanese chips first and from foreign manufacturers only as a last resort, Japanese firms start with advantages outside the theoretical "free-market" framework.

In addition, Japan's semiconductor firms are part of huge conglomerate empires. Relying on their deep pockets, and an accommodating government, Japanese companies have allegedly "dumped" excess chip production on world markets and have temporarily lost vast sums of money in the semiconductor industry. This initial stage is not unusual in a targeting strategy. If everyone loses money in the short term, "the winner is not the most efficient producer, but the one with the deepest pockets. Since the Japanese semiconductor companies are all part of huge conglomerates owned by major banks and ultimately backed by the Japanese government, theirs are deeper."[16]

"Free markets" in Japan differ from those envisioned in the USA, and specialization is not always the preferred strategy. In fact, none of the major industrialized countries believe in a theory of specialization to the extreme that is espoused in the United States. Japan, for example, is only one competitor nation that practices nonspecialized diversification. British, Italian, French, German, and Dutch corporations are busily diversifying – in scope as well as size. If international economies of scope exist, they will be made evident too late for firms in many of the most advanced and vital industries in the USA.

New businesses with large start-up costs and heavy research and development expenses are especially vulnerable to competitive pressures from large companies diversifying into their industry. American bioresearch firms fit into this category; research outlays are enormous and payoffs far into the future. Most biotechnology firms are relatively small, and probably only a handful will survive as independent companies. Meanwhile, the Japanese, erstwhile competitors of the USA, have targeted biotechnology as an industry with a key role to play in their world leadership strategy. Large capital outlays and distant rewards, both daunting attributes for US firms attuned to short-term results, play into the strengths of the Japanese. Accustomed to investing for the long term, Japanese firms patiently wait out modest interim results. Once more, most Japanese players in this emerging industry tend to be "huge corporations loaded with cash from their other operations."[17]

Because most domestic biotechnology companies are small and have few profitable products as yet to sustain them, they are handicapped in this respect. Extending the experience in semiconductors, only the very biggest and best prepared of the US biotechnology companies could withstand an ambitious policy of "targeting." Taking the long view, if the Japanese decide that acquisition is the only feasible means of entering the US market, they would be willing to pay the high price of participation in this high-technology field. Moreover, because of the overlap with the pharmaceutical business, another key area where the Japanese feel that a worldwide position requires a significant US presence, the "targeting" logically could extend to the basic drug industry itself.

In sum, what America's competitors do increasingly reverberates and influences US actions. For many decades, global competitive actions were ignored. In theory, extrapolating models of competition constructed for the domestic economy is still common; the rhetoric of textbooks and scholars has yet to catch up with reality. This, however, is typical; it is the rule rather than the exception that the explanation of business practices takes a retrospective view.[18]

When the USA played a dominant world role, this was tolerable, and business people suffered few real consequences from the misdirection of theory. In a world tilted less and less by US power, and challenged selectively on a number of fronts crucial to America's technological leadership, the stakes are much higher. The USA can no longer afford to shape national policy on outdated assumptions.

Specialization in business, for example, may remain valid in the limited time and space circumstances under which it originally was conceived. Much has changed since then. Business revolutions and evolutions have passed. Surely, specialization is not immune to change. Specialization is a structural characteristic, and structure follows strategy. After the innovations of a century and a half, specialization clearly needs reassessment as an all-encompassing strategy.

Large foreign competitors are obviously not marching to this single tune. Increasingly, foreign companies are combining large size with greater scope. For them to be proven wrong, the economies of scope would have to be negative. *Yet only a single objective argument has ever been raised against nonspecialized diversification*: managerial inefficiency arising from the complexities of diversification. This charge has often been made, but never demonstrated. In the following section, the managerial implications of becoming a more complex corporation are discussed.

Managerial Inefficiency

If all positive aspects of nonspecialized diversification were true *and without qualification*, every company would be diversified *in extremis*. This has not happened for two reasons.

1 Nonspecialized diversification has its time. Companies in pioneering and growth phases of their life-cycles *should not diversify*. Specialization is the simplest and therefore the best strategy, *when industry demand is growing*.
2 Even for mature businesses, niche strategies can succeed.

This leaves big companies in mature industries with declining rates of revenue growth as the logical candidates for nonspecialized diversification. This category of firms generally would be better positioned, if they diversified into a balance of risks and growth options, *all other things being equal*. However, other things seldom are equal, and managements may have little choice in some companies but to remain with their specialization. It offers the lesser evil, if management is ill equipped to handle complexity, and management cannot be replaced.

The mistakes of diversifiers who failed at the task of managing complexity serve as convenient examples for those mentally prepared to see the entire movement in a negative light. The positive potential from multi-industry diversification is seldom raised. Indeed, there is little interest in bringing attention to the existence of nonspecialized diversification as a separate strategy. Existing theory is built on specialization. Specialization defines efficiency, and that is all. To pose alternatives to specialization is to tug at one of the threads that tie the interwoven fabric of economic relationships together.

Alfred Chandler remarked on economists' peculiar omission of the study of the importance of administration to business strategy. It is as if a strategy, once chosen, becomes hostage to an administrative system that is unable to accommodate any higher order of complexity. This implied inflexibility is flatly contradicted by the facts. In industry after industry, new administrative structures arose in the wake of strategic innovations. As Chandler showed, structure tends to follow strategy.

That is not to say that structure follows strategy in a smooth and fully complementary fashion. A complex strategy often begins in experimental and tentative fashion. The administrative reforms that follow are halting and experimental in turn. While entrepreneurs map grand new strategies, another generation of managers generally must construct the administrative systems to make them efficient. In the conglomerate waves of twenty and thirty years ago, empire-builders came first, then managers. Conglomerateurs were not skilled managers, or motivated to become so. They put together the deals and left others to devise the techniques of coordination and control.

Obviously, progress in this mode tends to be disjointed, rather than smooth and steady. As nonspecialized diversification spreads into more and more companies and industries, administrative progress either follows or the structures fall apart. This is true as well for companies that sought economies of scale at the turn of the century, and conglomerates that built sprawling enterprises in the 1950s and 1960s, and it remains valid in today's revolutionary strategy of restructuring and rebuilding conglomerates of the 1950s and 1960s.

It is worthwhile noting that of the nine industrial companies the Federal Trade Commission identified as prototype conglomerates, eight are still independent companies, and all are still in business.[19] Within this grouping, a mixture of managerial systems applies. Textron and Teledyne, two pioneering conglomerates, retain "loose" administrative structures, with liberal autonomy for each major business and a tremendous spread into many industry sectors. ITT, G + W, and Litton have divested many of their early acquisitions and refocused on fewer main lines of business. Colt Industries and FMC took steps to avoid hostile takeovers; after restructuring, both companies appear content, for the time being, to concentrate in the several different fields in which they are presently involved. White Consolidated Industries was acquired in 1986 by Sweden's Electrolux, while LTV is struggling under chapter 11 bankruptcy to return profitability to its core steel business.

In each of these conglomerate cases, managements and organizational structures evolved in an attempt to implement the strategy of nonspecialized diversification. Charles Bluhdorn of G + W, for example, was an inveterate accumulator, buying companies with a collector's passion, but with no greater rationale than to build a bigger collection.

Martin Davis, the current chief executive officer of G + W, is a more disciplined manager. One of his first moves as CEO of G + W was to sell the excess baggage that Charles Bluhdorn had acquired over the years. Focused now on three major, but entirely separate industry sectors, G + W's image in the business press has gone from disparagement to approval. Since Martin Davis took command in 1983, G + W has discontinued a myriad of operations in manufacturing and natural resources, while acquiring other companies to add to its three operating segments: entertainment (movies, TV productions, Madison Square Garden, and theatre circuits), financial services (consumer and commercial lending), and publishing/information services (educational, business, trade, and mass market services).

It is now common to hear references to a reduced spread of operations, as in G + W's case, to "focused" diversification. Tainted by excesses and bad press, "conglomerate" is not a term with which companies seek to identify. None the less, changing the name does not alter the fact. Nonspecialized diversification is a substitute term employed here to avoid the prejudice automatically attached to any company described as a conglomerate.

"Focusing" refers to a learning curve experience. Agglomerates, as the first conglomerates were sometimes referred to, represented the initial phase of nonspecialized diversification: a random buying of companies strictly on the basis of short-term financial reasoning. As the movement matured, and the more unwieldly enterprises were disassembled, attention turned to management. Learning from experience, a new generation of diversifiers spared themselves from the more flagrant excesses of random growth. Staking out fewer business arenas, companies avoided taking on too much complexity at once.

Rome was not built in a day. Nonspecialized diversification will not be mastered overnight. Of the eight industrial conglomerates in the 1969 FTC study that are still independent, all continue to evolve. If history repeats itself, companies like Textron and Teledyne, with a great number of loosely administered businesses, have a distance to go, and probably more than one change in top management, before settling into a more tightly managed structure organized around fewer industry sectors. In short, developing a new management style occurs over a long period of time and after much experimentation. If the basic strategy of nonspecialized diversification was flawed, organizational performance eventually would suffer. Creative administration alone cannot offset a bad strategy. But if the strategy persists and becomes permanent, as is the case for many nonspecialized diversifiers, then administrative improvements implicitly follow.

In surveying the number of widely diversified firms, it is remarkable that so innovative a strategy resulted in so few fatalities. As this book is being written, the most glaring disasters of mismanagement have occurred in singularly undiversified corporations: banking (Bank of America, First Chicago, and Continental Illinois are prominent examples of mismanagement), savings and loans (the list is so long that the federal government's insurance system is itself near technical bankruptcy), and energy-related companies (the drop in energy prices forced many small- and medium-sized companies into bankruptcy).

Where the potential for unpleasant surprises remains highest is among the unmanaged but financially-controlled conglomerate empires created through leveraged buyouts. Run as classic holding companies, the leveraged buyouts' managing partners have no knowledge or hands-on experience with the collection of companies they control. Were advocates of "free markets" not so enamored of the virtues of unchecked market forces, they might perceive some of the managerial limitations they deemed so damaging to the health of earlier species of conglomerates. They might also see the inconsistency in championing LBOs as an expression of freedom in the marketplace, while remaining mute about the inefficiencies created by reverting to a passive holding-company type of control.

If the separately-managed business controlled through leveraged buyouts hit an economic trough, what management glue will hold them together? Mortgaged to the hilt, they are even less prepared to weather an economic storm than were their conglomerate predecessors who, whatever their shortcomings, were managed as a single operating and administered corporation. If early "operating" conglomerates were precariously structured and thereby vulnerable to managerial inefficiencies, then financially-oriented holding-company conglomerates formed through leveraged buyouts face a harsh day of reckoning indeed.

Failure to distinguish between managed and passive organizational structures (see chapter 2) contributes to an arbitrary lumping of all nonspecialized diversifiers into a single category. This confuses managing diversity with merely investing in companies. Further, it uses the management sins of one type of organization to condemn all the others. A stubborn insistence that nonspecialized complexity simply cannot be managed lacks conviction in the face of the many such companies that are managing. In contrast to US firms, conglomerates and cartel-like organizations are common in Japan and Europe. The Anglo-Dutch Unilever Company, Switzerland's Nestlé, and the UK's Hanson Trust are a few examples of companies already widely diversified, but who are still actively adding to their spread of businesses. Nestlé, for instance, already the world's largest diversified "food" company, with annual sales of roughly $26 billion (*c.*1988), has bundles of cash it is anxious to put to work. After digesting the $3 billion acquisition in 1985 of America's Carnation Company, plus assorted lesser acquisitions, Nestlé is currently on the prowl for more acquisitions.

By continually extending their frontiers, corporations grow and gain relative power. The process of evolution and change is continuous. In a single world economy, being big only in a home country means losing global competitive advantage. Similarly, being *merely* big lacks the advantage of size plus scope. In a progressively competitive world marketplace, the winners must innovate or fall behind. Specialization, as critical as it still is as a business-level strategy, is ill designed as a total corporate-level strategy for the modern global enterprise.

The Strategy of Nonspecialized Diversification

Composition into a nonspecialized firm embodies the four competitive elements previously described: centralized expertise at the corporate level, available and lower cost of capital, alternative internal investment options, and contestability with foreign nonspecialized corporations. Each factor represents a potential benefit from nonspecialization. To reach full potential, however, requires effective management. Without conscious effort at management, a nonspecialized organization would rely on a largely inert advantage from controlling a multiplicity of independent businesses. In such a passive organization, the nonspecialized firm tends to resemble a pure holding company, with all the attendant limitations. Separating holding-company diversification from the more successful "operating" mode is administrative decision-making at the top. This means proactive management. The corporate level must bring a competence that can be diffused throughout its members; it must create synergy, in other words. Although an abused word, having suffered from association with the first conglomerate movement, synergy is used here simply to mean an incremental value due to joining in a business family that each business could not, or would not, have realized on its own.

The two types of synergy that are possible in nonspecialized diversification are synergy from better cash management and synergy from better asset management. Each is discussed briefly below and in more detail in my book *Managing the Unmanageable*.[20]

Synergy From Cash Management

Cash management offers the easiest path to synergy for a company just starting to diversify. It was the route identified with the conglomerates formed by entrepreneurs in the 1950s and 1960s, where empire-building took precedence over empire-managing.

Financial synergy is energized by combining a mix of businesses with offsetting or complementary characteristics. The familiar portfolio matrix of the Boston Consulting Group with its four groupings of cows, stars, new ventures, and dogs (figure 4.1) illustrates cash-flow management among different types of businesses. By shifting moneys judiciously from cash-rich to cash-needy businesses in growing markets, the centrally-administered multi-business firm maximizes resource allocation within its miniature capital market.

No financial synergy exists in a passive holding-company structure, by comparison. Businesses stand alone, denying them the benefits of cash management so as to maximize the enterprise as a whole. Moreover, because each business must weather its own storms, the tolerance for

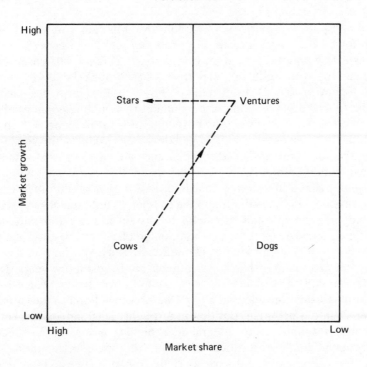

Figure 4.1 Portfolio matrix

miscalculations in the projected performance of acquired businesses in a pure holding company is minimal. Companies must be able to justify fully their price of acquisition from financial benefits alone: that is, reduction of overall risk, use of tax losses, or other financially-oriented advantages. Also, these types of financial benefits must outweigh the substantial premiums above market prices that one company generally pays to acquire another.

Thus, although a viable case for financial gains can be made under either an operating or a passive multi-business structure, by itself this latter type of synergy has its limitations. It cannot justify acquisitions that lack financial leverage, like firms in mature industries that are bought by companies in equally mature industries, where neither financial nor performance characteristics promise to make up for the acquisition premium paid to acquire the company's stock. To derive the synergy from such deals the acquirer has to "create" value in the acquired firm. This involves more than financial synergy. It requires a transference of management competence, either in a specific way, or in a general management sense, to the new business or businesses.

Synergy From Asset Management

The second path to synergy is to exploit an undermanaged aspect of an acquired business. In such cases, acquirers can seek to raise performance by transferring a particular parent-company competence, such as marketing, technology, or production expertise. Chesebrough–Pond's (now part of the Unilever Group) acquisition of Ragu in 1969 provides such an example. A mere $44 million in stock bought this small regional producer of spaghetti sauce. The acquisition raised questions at the time. Why move an old-line company specializing in personal-care products into the highly competitive food business? And why pick such an unlikely target with such seemingly limited potential?

Chesebrough–Pond's strategy encompassed a combination of transferring marketing skills to capitalize on the company's undermanaged product potential, plus an infusion of capital to sustain a successful build-and-expand program. The basis for significant differential advantage was the way Ragu's basic spaghetti product was marketed. Ragu spaghetti sauce revenues were $25 million when it was purchased. In just a few years, Ragu became *the* leading spaghetti sauce, accounting for nearly two of every three purchases nationwide, parlaying Chesebrough–Pond's modest initial investment into a dominant position in a roughly $600 million market.

Financial resources were integral to achieving a synergistic effect in Chesebrough–Pond's acquisition of Ragu: that is, investment in new capacity was necessary to gain market share. Financial resources generally are a part of diversification strategy, but money alone is an insufficient formula for success. If it were, acquired companies could borrow the funds to reap the rewards themselves. Moreover, if financial synergy alone could produce such results, then the performance of financial conglomerates should be much better than their record. The added key element is the transference of a specific management competence from the parent to the acquired company.

In entering new businesses, companies must seek a distinctive advantage. They should form strategic groups in businesses where they can leverage their strengths and leave those areas in which competitors enjoy a considerable edge. In the process, a substantial reshuffling of assets will ensue, stretching over many years, until the desired groupings are achieved.

Profitability will provide the pressure for corporations to specialize, a principle as old as business itself. In this case, however, the objective is not product specialization, but specialization of managerial resources within particular broad market segments. With varying degrees of managerial skills, companies will strive for different characteristics in their strategic groups. Desirable competitive arenas for one company can be undesirable for others.

General Electric, for instance, agreed in 1983 to sell its small housewares operations to Black and Decker. For General Electric, this furthered its strategic plan to emphasize high-growth and high-technology areas. For Black and Decker, the advantages were a major step up in size, a strong position in small household appliances, and the diversification it had been seeking to broaden its product base away from dependence on power tools.

When Dow Chemical bought Richardson-Merrell's ethical drug line, it viewed it as an alternative to the commodity side of its chemical business. Richardson-Merrell saw it as an opportunity to escape a field that had given it repeated headaches, low profits, and required a greater investment in research and development to remain competitive than the company could afford. Moreover, Richardson-Merrell traditionally did much better with its well-known over-the-counter brand names like Vicks and Oil of Olay. Subsequently, Dow expanded its prescription drug business and Richardson-Merrell devoted more money to improve earnings in its over-the-counter line.

This type of cross-switching into and out of businesses can be beneficial to both parties. It is a matter of capitalizing on company strengths and avoiding areas of weakness or marginal importance.

In sum, synergy comes in a variety of forms, just as diversification itself. Financial synergy is the easiest to achieve, but it is also the strategy with the lowest long-term payout. Managerial infusions into new businesses – a second order of synergy – can be achieved by transference of a parent company's special competence into an acquired firm. This stops short of a major overhaul or integration of acquired operations, but it can provide the stimulus for a rebirth of growth and expansion.

Synergy From Systems Management

The final, ultimate goal of successful diversification is to attain an ease and proficiency in assimilating and managing new businesses into an existing organization. Achieving this goal implies mastery of the art of managing diversity in a total systems sense. It suggests a diversified company operating in several different fields, yet unified into a single purposeful organization. This apex of diversification success eludes first-time diversifiers, nor is it a realistic goal for all companies. It makes the greatest demands on managerial ability, suggesting competence in strategic planning, organizational stucturing, and efficient corporate-level management of a diversified combination of businesses. Clearly, all companies are not equally gifted in handling this variety of tasks. Even where successful, creating capability for coordinated management and control of a diversified organization can take many, many years to master.

General Electric is perhaps the model of a company that has successfully diversified on a grand scale. With major structural and cultural adjustments now behind it, General Electric is as tightly managed as most single businesses. Despite General Electric's tremendous range of diversification, it has been able to absorb large acquisitions with barely a ripple in its administrative structure: for example, insurance (from Texaco in 1984), investment banking (Kidder Peabody in 1986), as well as RCA in 1986. The advantage of being a dynamic, very diversified firm is the ability to acquire new businesses with a minimum of reaction from a dominant culture that resists change.

In sum, nonspecialized diversification holds promise, but only if it can be managed. Until a company can learn to manage its acquisitions effectively, it is dependent on largely autonomous units operating profitably enough on their own to overcome the lack of administrative coordination. In the early stages, nonspecialization has attributes of a passive holding company. This leaves the firm vulnerable to unexpected downturns in new businesses that it does not yet firmly control or understand. Over time, the level of administrative competence will improve. Assuming mastery of this aspect of diversification, an optimum family of businesses can evolve and the fruits of the labor of diversification can be enjoyed. General Electric provides a role model that shows that it can be done. Other diversifiers seem certain to survive and imitate General Electric's example.

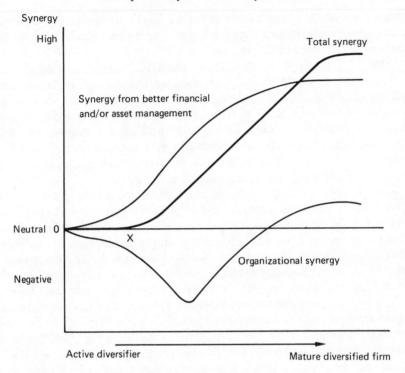

Figure 4.2   Conceptual diagram of synergy potential

An Illustration of the Tradeoffs in Nonspecialized Diversification

Figure 4.2 illustrates how synergy may develop in a diversified firm over many years. As the firm's journey beings, acquisitions strain its organizational structure. Administrative costs and frictions multiply. The more aggressively a firm diversifies, the greater the organizational diseconomies. In figure 4.2, the negative impact of organizational restructuring is eventually compensated for by the positive gains from improved financial and/or asset management.

Point X signifies the time when financial and/or asset-type synergies begin to overcome the effects of reorganization. From this point, the positive aspects of diversification begin to outweigh the initial negative impact of loss of administrative coordination and control.

Of course, actual synergy curves in a real firm may evolve in many different ways. Diversification could conceivably have a net positive impact from the start. Or point X, where the trade-offs in synergy begin to favor diversification, can come earlier or later. Where administrative diseconomies continue to frustrate management's ambitions, diversification can result in divestitures or liquidations.

Figure 4.2 portrays the sum of all the synergy outcomes of a firm's various acquisitions. In actuality, each acquisition will have its own distinct synergy curve, and be either of the financial or asset variety. Moreover, the combined synergistic effect of a continuous strategy of diversification can change over time as organizations add or divest businesses, and shift diversification strategy. For firms that continue and become mature multibusiness enterprises, the route will have been discontinuous, as opposed to the smooth curves shown in this simplified diagram.

RJR–Nabisco provides a classic example of the uneven path already traveled by many large, mature, and diversified companies. Starting from tobacco, RJR–Nabisco first entered the energy and ocean shipping businesses – in an apparent effort to capture the benefits represented by the Boston Consulting Group's portfolio matrix for optimizing cash management: that is, transferring tobacco's excess cash into higher-risk, higher-profit ventures. However, RJR brought no special competence to either field – and exposed itself to considerable managerial uncertainty, should either business falter. Subsequently, RJR divested itself of these businesses and made a series of investments and divestments in consumer businesses: acquiring Del Monte, Heublein, and Nabisco, and selling off wine, fast food, soft drinks, and other nonstrategic fits. A new chief executive of RJR–Nabisco, the former chief executive of Nabisco, contemplated a leveraged buyout that would make RJR–Nabisco a private company, and would involve selling off food businesses to pay down debt and to concentrate once again on tobacco; or selling the tobacco business to concentrate on food. Management's bid for the company failed, however, in the face of a higher offer from Kohlberg Kravis Roberts. RJR–Nabisco currently is a private company owned by Kohlberg Kravis Roberts, but even now its odyssey in terms of evolution and change is unlikely to stop at its present mixture of food and tobacco products.

In total, RJR's bumpy transition defies classic textbook examples of smooth corporate diversification, yet it is but one among many firms that "feel" their way into the future. "Old" diversifiers like G + W, Textron, ITT, FMC, Litton, etc. have shifted strategies often in the past in response to a new executive's vision, to pressures from environmental forces, or to fierce global competition. These types of strategic shocks defy precise forecasts and the best-laid plans. Yet the mid-course corrections they trigger have a dramatic strategic impact.

Eventually, if a company survives, a diversified mix of businesses emerges, enabling all the advantages of scope and a hospitable setting in which to operate. Coincidentally, management's goal of growth and survival of the firm is enhanced. The confluence of desired outcomes becomes possible generally after a long trial-and-error process. Managing the evolutionary changeover is the tricky part.

Clarifying the Meaning of Nonspecialized Diversification

Strictly interpreted, specialization would confine companies to a single product. Obviously, companies have not followed this prescription. Successively, firms have drawn further and further apart from a narrow specialization. First, companies diversified into related products and businesses, with specialization still providing the economic justification, because these moves could be rationalized as closely tied to skills used in the old business. When companies next diversified into different industries, not primarily to capitalize on the existing skills of specialization, but to enter new markets affording higher growth, the connection to specialization was essentially broken. The proclivity by managements toward greater diversification has been too obvious a trend to ignore. To remain credible, the principle of specialization needed to be reinterpreted, and the strict standard made more flexible.

Also, the concept of specialization never fitted well in the case of acquisitions, except when acquisitions were horizontal: for example, the acquired company was in the same line of business. In that particular instance, overlapping functions and personnel could be consolidated and costs reduced. If acquired companies were in different businesses, however, opportunities for consolidation and traditional cost reduction evaporated.

Moreover, combining business activities works at cross purposes when a firm diversifies in order to reduce dependence on a single business. The more a firm moves to tie its businesses together, at least in the short term, in terms of common activities, processes, or facilities, the more closely a company tends to resemble what it was, rather than design a new organization of what it wants to become.

There is, naturally, a desirability to limit the complexities of managing by containing the range of diversification attempted in a given span of time. Thus, a company with roots in soaps and detergents, like Procter & Gamble, may elect to diversify within a "consumer-goods" context. This focuses its horizons in one sense, but opens the possibility for acquisitions in fields fundamentally different from its traditional soaps and detergents: an example of this is the acquisition of Norwich Eaton, an over-the-counter drug maker, and Richardson-Vicks (the old Richardson-Merrell), a maker of over-the-counter health and beauty products.

Similarly, United Technologies is widely diversified within an "industrial-products" orientation, whereas companies like American Express and

Sears are broadly diversified within "services." This focusing of diversification allows companies to move away from a single product or single line of products, yet avoid random moves in any direction.

Containment of diversification reduces the task of managing complexity. The further afield a company reaches, the more adjustments corporate-level management must make, and the more difficult overall management becomes. Trade-offs must be made between managerial inefficiency arising from facing too much unaccustomed complexity and the potential limitation from remaining close to an industry where growth is slowing or where a company lacks a competitive advantage.

This is the message of figure 4.2. Too much diversification too fast can cause corporate indigestion. Yet staying in a business that offers limited growth can be fatal. As firms acquire familiarity coping with the complexities of diversification, the spread of activities can, and should, widen.

Clinging to specialization as the only explanation for diversification misreads history and managerial intent over the past several decades. Managements have acquired new businesses for many reasons, but the sharing of facilities or the combination of functional departments – the criteria suggested by Michael Porter – could hardly be high in priority. Buying entire companies, each complete with its staff departments and operating systems, is not the classical mode in which specialization was pictured. In the 1920s and 1930s, companies diversified from the inside out into related businesses by using internal research and development skills. DuPont leveraged its expertise in chemicals to develop new products/markets in fibers, film, and plastics. US Rubber similarly relied on in-house research technology to diversify into chemicals. This style of diversification from within allowed companies to expand into new products and markets without sacrificing close managerial supervision in the process.

Today's diversification is into less-related businesses and is accomplished primarily through acquisitions. Here, neither internal skills nor shared resources are the main motivators, nor can managerial supervision be as tight. To argue that specialization retains a customary starring role, while corporate practices have dramatically shifted, sounds hollow. It amounts to denying the legitimacy of actions by hundreds and hundreds of companies.

Mistakes unquestionably have been made. Unrelated acquisitions that should never have been made have failed. These are the normal statistics of change. In static equilibrium, a good theory is ageless. In reality, conditions constantly alter and explanations must adjust or become irrelevant.

The theory of specialization needs to adjust to current conditions. Its role is as crucial as ever; specialization is still a key to the success of individual businesses, but it is not necessarily a key to corporate strategy. When a firm elects to diversify away from a single or narrow specialization, it cannot rely on its business managers for guidance. Separating business from corporate strategy is an area where both managers and academics need to devote more study.

Suggestions for Improved Results from Nonspecialized Diversification

Management and economic theories often ignore the "what is" of business practice. Instead, theories build on hypotheses based on "what isn't" and pass it off as close enough. Neither ignorance of what business does, nor slavish imitation of business practices is likely to lead to an understanding of how business can do better.

Current practices of management are far from perfect, and imperfect theories are more likely to mislead than instruct. What is needed is a mid-course that gives managers new guidelines that are consistent with business history, empirical observations, and common sense.

There can never be iron-clad formulae for success. None the less, ways to improve the record for nonspecialized diversifiers can be ventured, based on many case histories of both successes and failures. Several points stand out; in particular, the following five elements are important for managements to consider before diversifying. In company after company, implementation of a strategy of nonspecialized diversification floundered because one or more of the suggestions below was insufficiently studied or understood.

Choose the Right People

People are the chief inhibiting factor for dynamic change. Deciding to alter the basic way a company does business, for example, while retaining the same people at the top who built the present company in their image is a recipe for failure. At the corporate level, where diversity needs to be coordinated and managed, having the wrong mind-set assures future problems of execution. This suggests a turnover or reassignment of top managers who are unable or unwilling to accommodate to rapid change before taking the first serious move to diversify.

The top management team will oversee the transition toward becoming a nonspecialized company. To make a smooth changeover, top managers need to be open: willing to accept new challenges and new opportunities. They must be oriented to change, creating a different future rather than repeating the past. Without the proper attitude and orientation of the top management team, nonspecialized diversification will face enormous hurdles. Although the proper orientation in top management cannot guarantee success in diversification, without the right attitude the strategy will almost certainly fail.

Armco offers an example of a firm that diversified, but kept a rigid conservative style. Unprepared to operate in a financial-services market, Armco's engineering mind-set forced it back into the steel business. The transition from steel to financial services would have been extremely difficult at best. Without a change in mental attitude – suggesting new faces and reassignments of existing personnel – the failed outcome was predictable.

Top managers who spend a career in one industry seldom do well in executing a changeover strategy. That is not always a fault of the individual managers, who may be excellent in their specialty. Often, the organizational system is to blame. Line managers who rise through the ranks ultimately reach the top business rung, at which point they fall victim to the Peter Principle: they are promoted to the corporate level and beyond the business level, where they are most competent. Having been indoctrinated in running a particular business, they are now asked to be broad-gauge managers and develop strategy for the survival of the entire firm. This asks more of some managers than they have to give. In a single-industry setting, the top job obviously demands less of a change in managerial style than in a very diversified firm. One of the most difficult challenges for managers is to oversee the change from being a one-industry company to becoming a multi-form organization. Exceptional management powers are needed. Trying to undertake this magnitude of change only with personnel that have been steeped in a single tradition for their entire working lives is making a difficult task virtually impossible.

During the mid-1980s, the chief executive of Alcoa determined to set a different course for this old-line industrial powerhouse in the aluminum business. The chief executive boldly forecast that by 1995 Alcoa would realize only half of its sales from the aluminum business. Yet only two years after being promoted to head the company, Alcoa's board of directors replaced him. The next designated top manager steered Alcoa back to its core aluminum business, where he is convinced the company should stay.

A number of factors contributed to this aborted evolution at Alcoa. The complete story may never be fully revealed. Of what is publicly known, it is clear that the board of directors either did not clearly grasp, or were unsympathetic to, the specifics of the drive to diversify. Perhaps more fundamental, as expressed in an article on Alcoa's failed foray into diversification, is the enormous amount of inertia built into a company that big and that conservative: "[Alcoa] ran afoul of the company's deeply ingrained corporate culture. Century-old Alcoa, with $7.7 billion in annual sales, is the antithesis of the young, risk-oriented company."[21]

If diversification was to have any chance at all in Alcoa's circumstances, a reorientation in top management was an essential preliminary step. A company burdened with so much tradition cannot at the same time hope to execute successfully one of the most difficult of corporate maneuvers. Along with senior managers, the board of directors must come on board. Their backing and commitment is crucial for a firm to weather the inevitable ups and downs of a long transitional period. Until and unless the ones charged with responsibility for policy share a vision of the company's future, a company starts its diversification program facing very long odds.

Unfortunately, an internal solution is not always possible. The persons responsible for leading the company may be the same ones that handicap a successful transition. Although ineffectiveness at the top can be relatively easy to diagnose, there is seldom an easy cure. In these cases, a company remains stuck in neutral. For better or worse, survival for the Armcos and Alcoas of this world depends on their core business. This can work out, if the core business remains healthy, but it signifies a victory of accident over planning. If diversification was the strategy of choice, then failing to execute it, regardless of how the future profitability of the company turns out, cannot be disguised as good strategic management.

In abandoning diversification, Alcoa imposes a difficult alternative on its top managers: to reduce the size of the corporation. As in other mature materials and resource businesses, tremendous changes have taken place in the domestic aluminum business over the years. United States aluminum producers have been squeezed by explosive growth in aluminum capacity world-wide, a substantial portion of which is state-controlled and therefore protected from free-market forces. Moreover, substitution of aluminum by other materials has decreased its use in major industries like automobiles, while at the same time the amount of aluminum to produce the same number of products for customers like soft-drink and beer bottlers has shrunk dramatically. As summed up by Alcoa's vice-president for corporate planning: "In a postindustrial society, materials intensity is not where it's at."[22] If Alcoa cannot go "where it's at," it will be forced to oversee the shrinking of the corporation, an action that goes against corporate managers' basic instincts for growth and survival.

The one inhibiting factor above all others in moving toward higher levels of diversification nationwide, and globally, is managerial competence. That restraint keeps companies that should change from changing, and some that have tried changing from succeeding. The exceptional skills required for multi-business management are not evenly distributed among the corporate population. Those companies endowed with superior gifts of management will – in an open market – seek out opportunities where their skills may be used to best advantage. Within a normally distributed set of skill levels, the better-managed companies will survive and raise competitiveness and efficiency in the economy by acquiring underperforming companies that either cannot, or will not, change with the times.

Choose the Right Structure

Current organizational structures were designed to assure strong control from the top. The multidivisional structures illustrated in management textbooks evolved from frameworks adapted for tightly-managed single businesses. As companies diversified, product divisions replaced functional departments, and business groups eventually replaced product divisions. Meanwhile, the hierarchical manner of governance has been slow to adapt. Despite general recognition that more diversification demands greater autonomy at the business level, corporate headquarters have only recently loosened their grip. There is a considerable distance to go in finding a proper middle ground between corporate-wide cohesion and business-level autonomy.

As a hangover from using old pyramidal structures, corporations still tend to be tall instead of flat. Corporate personnel still intermingle excessively with business operations. The reluctance to take the necessary steps is understandable in terms of its human consequences. As companies diversify and their control over operational units loosens, layers of middle corporate managers become redundant.

Corporate managements need to slim down at the same time that business units are operating more like separate companies. This does not imply diminished importance of the corporate level; it simply recognizes that the two levels have different responsibilities in a diversified organization. The chief corporate task is to plot the future course for the corporation as a whole, and to review and monitor the businesses it controls. For their part, business managers must have maximum freedom to make competitive decisions, while being held accountable for results. These simple principles are uncontested as good theory, but companies lack the discipline to carry them out in practice. Part of the reason is structural. Instead of separate headquarters, corporate- and business-level top managers tend to work out of the same offices. This dilutes the effectiveness on both sides. Business heads spend time trying to influence corporate-level decisions, while corporate-level officers get involved in operational details.

The two levels of management should be physically separate from one another. Business heads in charge of operations need to work and identify with their businesses. They must give their full effort toward building the most efficient business, and be measured by their progress in meeting that goal. Only by thinking and acting as chief executives of their own firms can business managers in a multi-business organization achieve the same dedication and efficiency as the single companies with which they compete. Within each major business, vertical communications between managers and employees will foster a greater team effort from top to bottom. This demands the physical presence of business-level executives in the field, rather than at the headquarters office.

Horizontal communications, meanwhile, between the business and corporate levels need to be established as well. This can be accomplished through periodic meetings of top corporate- and business-level managers. Appointing business heads to key corporate committees, in addition to automatic membership on a corporate-wide policy committee, are ways to keep everyone informed and pulling in the same direction. Reforms are needed, in other words, that allow major business units to act like free-standing companies as much as possible – thus competing with maximum flexibility within their markets – while developing a common philosophy and sharing of organizational goals at the top.

Delegating authority to the business level means keeping the corporate staff lean. Left unchecked, corporate staffs have a way of proliferating paperwork and reports. Unless it is consciously monitored, employee growth at the nonproducing corporate level tends to outstrip growth at the producing business level. At General Electric, arguably one of the best-run companies, a review of corporate-level output revealed that:[23]

1 every quarter General Electric was sending out reports on injuries and illness in the company that went to 2,300 people!
2 eight people at headquarters were billing various costs back and forth among headquarters components;
3 there were 565 reporting components that sent in certain reports every quarter: Semiconductor – one of GE's smaller businesses – had 31 reporting components which translated to 1,200 closing reports addressed to headquarters.

As shown in figure 2.1 above, companies actively diversifying need to adapt transitional organizational structures. Depending on the type of strategy, and the ambition of its diversification program, a company can either relax or tighten the degree of autonomy given to business units. In a fast-paced, active diversification program, for example, rigid organizational control clearly would be inappropriate. Organizational lines of command drawn too tightly would work against the basic strategy of adaptation and change. As corporations approach their desired range of diversification, and fervor for additional diversification slackens, more stable organizational structures can follow.

A common failing of early conglomerates was to spread themselves across too many businesses far too quickly. Without a schedule or plan for assimilating acquisitions, companies focused almost entirely on buying rather than managing. Diversification without an administrative mechanism in mind raised the risk of managerial failure. Managerial resources were stretched thin without compensating gains in operating efficiencies. US Industries, a sprawling conglomerate of the 1960s, absorbed more than one hundred smallish companies in short order. It carried decentralization to an extreme. A simple premise that entrepreneurial companies could be bought and left to operate as before was exposed as a simplistic idea in the following decade.

Unfortunately, organizational theory is at present infrequently joined with organizational strategy. The few design prototypes for structure tend to fix on three or four primary variants, all in existence for at least half a century. Moreover, traditional fixed structures imply organizational stability. None of the designs typically illustrated in textbooks were designed with change in mind. There is no structural accommodation, in other words. for going from state to state. Especially in large complex organizations, the contribution of administration to strategy tends to be overlooked. How did multi-businesses make the journey from simple to complex organizations? The answer will not be found in a textbook. Nor have managements yet devised a unanimity of views on how best to get from here to there.

Change the Environment

Finally, if a company desires to change its profile, it should consider relocating corporate headquarters. A dramatic change in strategy suggests a dramatic change in culture. And companies wanting to cut old cultural trappings have a better chance, if they change their traditional cultural setting. But culture is like the weather: many complain, but few do anything about it. One of the exceptions is RJR–Nabisco. The new chief executive – formerly the head of Nabisco – moved the firm from its tobacco stronghold in Winston-Salem, North Carolina to a new headquarters in Atlanta, Georgia. Once RJR–Nabisco had been committed to break with its past as an old-line tobacco company, the chief executive moved to shape its future by distancing the company from everyday reminders of its past. Leaving Winston-Salem made a clear statement that would not have been as credible had RJR–Nabisco stayed in tobacco country.

Similarly, numerous industrial firms have grown up and remained in localities identified with their heritage: Pennsylvania for steel, aluminum, and coal; Michigan for automobiles; California for entertainment and leisure; and Texas for oil. The symbolism of a move of headquarters can be as important as the fact of the move itself. Handled properly, relocation offers the opportunity to recast the way the corporation thinks, while reorganizing internally to reorient the way an organization works.

Choose the Right Strategy

For companies that do not know what they want to become, any acquisition will do. This lack of strategic vision was the downfall of many conglomerates constructed in the 1950s and 1960s. One acquisition after another added up to a bigger company, but seldom a better one. Complexity overwhelmed financial synergies, which were the only potential synergies available from such an approach. Combining "a shipbuilder with an ice-cream manufacturer" – an example of extreme conglomerate-style diversification used by the Federal Trade Commission – proved to be neither instinctively sound nor good applied strategy for companies that tried such haphazard pairings.

Whenever possible, nonspecialized diversification should start with a firm's distinctive capabilities. Companies that excel in certain specific activities (marketing, production, distribution, organization, etc.) should leverage these skills to advantage. Similarly, companies good at managing in a broader sense, such as efficiency in cost containment, licensing arrangements, or international negotiations, should use these strengths to gain a competitive edge. Procter & Gamble and Philip Morris, for example, are regarded as excellent marketing companies; this area of competence has guided both firms toward acquisitions in consumer goods, where advertising, promotion, and brand segmentation are keys to success. Emphasis on these marketing skills allows entry into a wide range of different businesses, but at the same time restricts acquisitions to consumer-oriented companies. This measured reach prevents overextending a company's managerial capability. While easing the exit from old businesses, an old business "theme" remains. New businesses can still operate with autonomy, but both the parent corporation and its business partners share a strategic orientation.

This is an important difference from Michael Porter's idea of having acquirer and acquiree physically joined, grafting an acquisition to the parent, in effect, by combining departmental forces in specific areas like marketing or sales. Such tight integration would defeat the basic purpose of nonspecialized diversification. Moreover, instead of surveying a large population of potential new businesses to enter, a company's scope would extend only to those relatively isolated opportunities where a combination of activities is feasible.

In fact, in almost every nonspecialized acquisition, new businesses differ more than they resemble an acquirer's core business: that is, in terms of research and development emphasis, asset intensity, production processes, plant layout and process, etc. Thus, Procter & Gamble's diversification into over-the-counter drugs moved the company into a different industry, which had marked contrasts to soap and detergents, yet enabled Procter & Gamble to exploit its consumer marketing background as an aid in bridging this crossover into fundamentally new territory.

The essence of successful nonspecialized diversification involves cutting loose from industry-imposed restrictions, in order to escape core-business limitations, while using experience in the core business to alleviate transitional problems. Special skills are part of the diversification strategy, but they are not the whole part and, in the majority of actual cases, they are not the main part.

Diversification is a gradual process. Companies tend to diversify, assimilate, and diversify again. In the initial phases, a company is on a learning curve. Consequently, it must not attempt to ingest too much that is new. As the company gains experience, it can aspire to more venturesome moves.

Planning for change, in turn, demands methods that are different from planning for continuity. This distinction is seldom explicitly made. Instead, business-level planning attracts the lion's share of attention. Surveys of business managers seldom list separate questions for corporate-level and business-level planning. When asked, chief executives have revealed an eclectic approach to corporate-level planning, with heavy reliance on the chief executive's own instincts and experience as the major contributions to planning solutions.[24]

Chief executives tend to approach restructuring – through acquisitions, divestments, and reorganizations – in their own special way. Internal committees sometimes play an advisory role. Outside consultants and board of directors provide additional sources of input. Information can also come from the firm's corporate-planning department. Persons somewhere in a company are generally assigned responsibility to study corporate-wide moves, but the system is *ad hoc* rather than formal, and varies widely from firm to firm.

Principal attention to planning has been paid, and most progress has been made, in refining the annual planning routine that decides resource allocation among the various businesses. This is operational planning. A mountain of articles on how to be a better business planner are available, but hardly anything worthwhile exists on planning for change. Peculiarly, the most strategic of all planning, affecting the corporation's very survival, has been neglected during the most dynamic and unprecedented wave of restructuring in the nation's history. A survey by Booz, Allen, and Hamilton of firms represented in a *Business Week* conference on planning found that: "80% of the 145 participating firms indicated that they were dissatisfied with the poor results of their strategic planning."[25] While business planning has become more rigorous, corporate planning has suffered: "the widespread use of 'sophisticated' planning techniques has often been cited as a key contributor to the decline of innovation."[26]

Choose the Right Timing

"Buy no company before its time" is a motto that companies could live by. Diversifying too early or too late entails a special kind of risk. Companies in growing industries with opportunities for profitable reinvestment lack a compelling reason to diversify afield. A shift in strategy would pose managerial risks in exchange for a new but unknown investment outlet: a switch that offers less than what the company already enjoys. Diversifying too early also would divert managerial as well as financial resources from an attractive core business. Other things being equal, simple is better than complex, and running a business one knows is easier than learning a new one.

Diversifying too late, however, is the more common fault. Once a company's markets have been saturated and new product introductions become harder, a company's rate of growth starts to slow down. Immediately following the apex in sales growth, a company enjoys high expectations generated by its past performance, which generally means high stock price, maximum borrowing power at low rates, and an enviable reputation for excellence: all helpful traits in making acquisitions on favorable terms. Ideally, the peak of a company's life-cycle would be the time to prepare for the next stage of development. Few companies or individuals, however, are blessed with perfect foresight in anticipating the precise moment to act. Rather than try to forecast the exact timing for a change, a better strategy is to prepare a plan for action, with the expectation of being only approximately right on timing.

The best time to leave an industry is before being forced. In 1982, when a new chief executive took over at Arvin Industries, the main manufacturer of automobile exhaust systems, the company depended on the automobile industry for about 60 percent of sales and up to 70 percent of earnings. As the automobile industry declined, so did Arvin Industries. The company was closely wedded to its customer base and to the pressure exerted by a few very large domestic car manufacturers. Determined to spread business risks and raise corporate profitability, the new chief executive diversified into several new fields, guided in part by expertise in similar product categories and with several helpful acquisitions. Familiarity in the automobile heater business, for example, led Arvin Industries to become the largest producer of portable electric space heaters, opening a completely new market serving different customers. Car radios led the company into home radios and the consumer electronic business. The most venturesome and distant acquisition from Arvin Industries' core business was Calspan, originally Curtiss-Wright's aeronautical laboratory, which provided Arvin Industries a way into government, business, and nonprofit research and development contracts.

Once diversified, Arvin Industries then started pressing for new product introductions from its nonautomobile businesses. Combined with some niche acquisitions, Arvin Industries transformed itself from a mundane company tied to the vicious ups and downs of the automobile industry into an above-average performer in several different products and markets: automotive parts, household products, electronics, and research and development. When Arvin Industries' regeneration began, the new chief executive had hoped to add $100 million in sales by 1984. As it turned out, new sales amounted to $181 million in 1984, and nonautomobile revenues contributed 38 percent of operating profits.

Moreover, Arvin Industries did not neglect its automobile customers. The company retained a satisfactory base business in automobile parts, but, by diversifying, Arvin Industries set its own course and, in good strategic fashion, helped chart its own future, rather than being pulled in someone else's wake.

For giant companies that dominate their industries, like an Alcoa in aluminum or Exxon in oil, the best time to diversify has long since passed. These are yesterday's leaders. Their industry's relative standing has slipped, giving way to newcomers like computers, electronics, and information services. A transformation at this late date would be treacherous, although not impossible. United States Steel proved it could be done. As the nation's largest steel-maker, United States Steel took a high-risk gamble in diversifying away from steel. Still, diversification for most industrial giants poses severe obstacles. Too big to fail and too big to sell, these companies are stuck with oversize core businesses. To achieve balanced diversification, the core business must shrink, through plant closings, sale of assets, dismemberment, or liquidations. Such unpopular and politically difficult decisions are often postponed until forced on companies by harsh economic realities.

Timing the rate at which diversification progresses is likewise important. Companies that rapidly follow one acquisition with another and another, and pyramid borrowings in order to pay for them, are taking risks of another sort. Among the factors distinguishing sound diversification from random accumulation is a planned schedule of progression. A good deal of research and information should precede every important acquisition. This takes time. The right opportunity generally takes patient waiting. Also, normal business cycles tend to move stock prices higher or lower, influencing the timing for the right move at the right time. Finally, it takes several years after acquiring a company before it can be assimilated as a well-functioning part of the corporation. In sum, diversification needs to be taken at a sustainable pace. Otherwise, the complexities from combining basically unrelated businesses will outweigh whatever economic benefits might otherwise have been forthcoming.

Summary

In order for nonspecialized diversification to succeed, it must be appreciated, the strategy must be carefully formulated, and implementation must respect a few practical guidelines. These are not radical ideas. Few revolutionary ideas in strategic thinking have emerged since the mid-1950s. The evolution in administrative management mainly needs to catch up with strategic redirection that has already occurred.

In referring once more to the success of Japanese competition, one is struck less by its strategic vision than by an unrelenting emphasis on execution of relatively simple strategies. Having no biases against nonspecialized diversification, Japanese companies have followed what they see as a natural progression from declining to growing industries. On a practical level, the soundness of such an industrial policy seems obvious – even to many American managements and policy-makers. Yet in the United States there is considerable learned opposition to following the Japanese and European leads in diversification, even though the consequences of being wrong can be severe.

Unfortunately for United States' industrial policy, the actions of managers and policy-makers are influenced by an academic community that refuses to concede that it may be wrong, or that the theoretical underpinnings of more than two hundred years may need replacement.

Notes

1 Gordon Donaldson and Jay Lorsch, *Decision Making at the Top: The Shaping of Strategic Direction* (Basic Books, New York, 1983), p. 171.
2 Robert Heller, *The Naked Manager* (Truman Talley Books, E. P. Dutton, New York, 1985), p. 269.
3 Richard Schmalensee, "Remarks," in *The Conglomerate Corporation*, eds Roger D. Blair and Robert F. Lanzillotti (Oelgeschlage, Gunn & Hain, Cambridge, Mass., 1981), p. 336.
4 Richard Bettis and C. K. Prahaled, "The dominant logic: a new linkage between diversity and performance," *Strategic Management Journal*, 7 (1986), pp. 485–501, esp. p. 499.
5 Harold S. Geneen, "The strategy of diversification," in *Competitive Strategic Management*, ed. Robert Boyden Lamb (Prentice-Hall, Englewood Cliffs, NJ, 1984), pp. 401–2.
6 Richard S. Tedlow and Richard R. Johns, Jr, "Introduction," in *Managing Big Business*, eds Tedlow and Johns (Harvard Business School Press, Boston, Mass., 1986), p. xxi.
7 Lee Iaccoca, with William Novak, *Iaccoca: An Autobiography*, (Bantam, New York, 1984).
8 John Kitching, "Why do mergers miscarry?" *Harvard Business Review*, 45

(1967), pp. 84–101. Also cited by Oliver Williamson as a factor in many of his extensive writings on the subject. For a recent book see Oliver E. Williamson, *Markets and Hierarchies: Analysis and Antitrust Implications* (Macmillan, New York, 1975).

9 Donaldson and Lorsch, *Decision Making at the Top*, pp. 7, 50.

10 Ibid., p. 166.

11 *Business Week*, 1 February 1988, p. 50.

12 *Wall Street Journal*, 9 March 1987, p. 1.

13 *Wall Street Journal*, 6 June 1988, p. 6.

14 *Fortune*, 20 July 1987, p. 98.

15 *Business Week*, 30 December 1985, p. 48.

16 Clyde V. Prestowitz, former counselor on Japanese affairs to US Commerce Department Secretary, Malcolm Baldridge, in an editorial, *Wall Street Journal*, 26 September 1986, p. 30.

17 *Wall Street Journal*, 17 December 1987, p. 1.

18 The lag of educational theory behind business practice has been noted by several authors. See, for example, Oliver Williamson, "The multidivisional structure," in *Organizational Economics*, eds Jay B. Barney and William G. Ouchi (Jossey-Bass, San Francisco, Calif., 1986), p. 179; Peter F. Drucker, *Innovation and Entrepreneurship* (Harper & Row, New York, 1973), p. 265; Igor H. Ansoff, as cited in Milton Leontiades, *Strategies for Diversification and Change*, (Little, Brown, Boston, Mass., 1980), p. 2.

19 Federal Trade Commission, "Economic report on corporate mergers," staff report for the *Subcommittee on Antitrust and Monopoly of the Committee on the Judiciary, U.S. Senate, Pact 8A*, 1969, pp. 499–654. Two of the eleven companies cited as the "new conglomerates" – General American Transportation Corporation and General Telephone and Electronics – were not primarily industrial companies and therefore were not included with the nine other conglomerates that the FTC used to describe this new genre.

20 Milton Leontiades, *Managing the Unmanageable: Strategies for Success within the Conglomerate* (Addison-Wesley, Reading, Mass., 1986), pp. 48–69.

21 *Business Week*, 29 June 1988, p. 59.

22 *Business Week*, 25 February 1985, p. 114.

23 Dennis D. Dammerman, Senior Vice-President, Finance, General Electric, in a speech to GE's Delaware Valley FMP/ISMP (Financial Management Program/ Information Systems Management Program), 13 July 1988.

24 Conclusions are based on an unpublished survey of chief executive officers in more than one hundred major corporations. The survey was conducted by Milton Leontiades, Rutgers University, Camden, NJ, 1988.

25 John D. C. Roach, "From strategic planning to strategic performance: closing the achievement gap," *Outlook* (Spring 1981), p. 19.

26 Ibid., p. 24.

Epilogue

Business is about change. Theories of business are about statics. During the reformation in American business in the late 1980s – the most dramatic reformation since big business began in the United States – no up-to-date explanations have been forthcoming from academics that deal with the motivations for change. What theory exists is a 200-year-old view of "perfect competition:" an oxymoron that has little to do with competition or perfection.

A relatively new approach to competitive firm strategy, expounded most fully in the works of Harvard's Michael Porter, borrows extensively from a branch of economics – industrial organization economics – that, as conceived, ignores motivations of firm managers and, as applied, sees industry stability as the norm. Porter's revised perspective of industrial economics' model focuses almost exclusively on the business level rather than the corporate level, and on a firm strategy built around specialization. A company's core specialty, in effect, determines its future. Rigorously interpreted, no business should diversify away from its roots. If taken to heart by business managers, big businesses would eventually become an endangered species of corporate dinosaurs: allowed to grow, but not adapt. Economies of scale would be the strategy of choice, because only a bigger version of the same company would retain the advantages of specialization. Even allowing for *some* evolutionary shifts in industry structures over time, Michael Porter sees firm diversification only justified as an extension of existing skills or resources, such as more products through the same distribution channels, the sharing of sales people by two or more product lines, or shared production facilities in order to lower unit costs. Porter's is basically a cost-based strategy that mimics economics' emphasis on lowered costs as the only legitimate basis for expansion.

Lowered costs, however, are not what most diversification is about. The number of cost-motivated acquisitions are relatively few. Most companies clearly diversify in order to enter new businesses which, in the opinion of management, offer growth potential not possible by remaining specialized in the industry of which they are a part.

The distinctiveness of new businesses also precludes an "instant integration" with the parent that is implicit in Porter's strategy of "shared costs." After acquiring new businesses, a period of assimilation of different cultures and management styles is necessary to manage the total organization successfully. This period of changeover and transition is the most treacherous aspect of management to master. It affects the long-term survival of firms. Yet this is where theoretical guidance is lacking. Academics in economics and business refuse to prescribe for business patients with the most serious maladies. Should patients recover on their own, however, academics could prescribe one of the many "wellness" programs that the profession specializes in.

While companies are earnestly seeking guidance on how to navigate their futures, academic researchers are dedicated to constructing an ideal environment, whether or not it applies to business. Unfortunately, this is not a Panglossian world. Economic futures are made; they do not just happen. History is the only predictable vision. And it is a simple view of a long-past historical setting that remains ageless in models of business behavior and acts as a barrier to real change.

A preoccupation with perfection blinds one to reality. In teaching, as an example, the neatness of exact models that produce predictable outcomes makes it easier for instructors to teach, although precision is gained at the expense of knowledge. The Carnegie- and Ford-sponsored studies of higher education in business recommended business cases as primary teaching tools in business policy courses. Each business case takes a unique situation and analyzes the problems within the particular industry and competitor settings. Given sufficient experience in dealing with problem-solving in a variety of business situations, general frameworks for analyzing firm behavior under certain conditions are possible. Nevertheless, there is a tremendous variety of possible outcomes within such loose frameworks of analysis. For example, companies in the same industry that are approximately equal in resources may decide on opposite strategies, a not uncommon happening played out many times in the past: IBM vs the seven dwarfs in computers; McDonald's vs Howard Johnson in fast-food; K-Mart vs W. T. Grant in discount merchandising; and, more recently, Sears vs Penney in mass merchandising; and RJR–Nabisco vs Philip Morris in tobacco/food.

The case method is inimical to strict scientific method. Yet it is unrealistic to expect instructors with neither an applied business education, nor experience in business firms, nor motivation to relate the theory of business to its real-life image, to favor business cases over business models. The pressure by universities for their faculty to publish in the most abstract journals pushes business schools to follow the path taken by "economic science." Lacking external pressures for change, business schools are likely to place a higher premium on satisfying the internal goals of administrators and faculty, rather than their clients: students and business firms.

The risk of a backlash is real. Business firms already run their own training centers. Increasingly, businesses feel compelled to teach what universities fail to deliver. In General Electric's Management Development Institute in Croton-on-Hudson, New York, for example, the mission is to make managers "more action-oriented, more risk-oriented, more people-oriented."[1] These qualities cannot be taught through scientific models alone. There are aspects, in truth, that only actual organizational experience may be able to provide. However, the distance between business education and business careers has been allowed to widen to where businesses may have little alternative but to move to fill the growing void.

The implication for business education is not necessarily a lesser emphasis on business education. Conceivably, business education could prosper alongside a growing independent system of business training. Familiarity with quantitative tools, accounting systems, and principles of marketing, finance, organization, etc. will remain important building blocks for competency in managing a business. Minimum skill levels will continue to be demanded by business firms for graduates from business schools. Of more questionable value is the teaching of generic techniques of science without regard to their application to business firms. The curricula in top business schools emphasize those technical skills that define the faculty who are its most accomplished researchers and also determine the promotability and tenurability of junior faculty. This emphasis tends to formalize the subject matter to a degree where the analytical techniques become the main focus and comprehension of the topic gets lost in a maze of diversionary and unhelpful symbols.

The imminent danger for business schools is a loss of influence. The more divorced business education becomes from policy issues, the less policy-makers will tend to rely on advice given by those only armed with a formal education.

For academic economists, an eclipse in policy influence is already perceptible. In their most visible policy role – the President's Council of Economic Advisers – the influence of economists has noticeably waned. Since Walter Heller served as President Kennedy's Chairman of the Council of Economic Advisers in the early 1960s, the regard for the Council's policy advice has steadily eroded. Under President Reagan, the role of chief economic adviser openly shifted to James Baker, formerly the President's Chief of Staff and later Secretary of the Treasury. Soon after the 1988 presidential election, president-elect George Bush made a public announcement that his chief economic adviser would be James Baker once again, although Baker officially would serve as the President's Secretary of State in the new administration.

In choosing to be seen as scientists, academic economists have forfeited their claim to be taken seriously as policy advisers. What credibility they retain as business commentators is due in large measure to the deference paid to them by television and print media, which are apparently unable to make a meaningful distinction between economics and business. Erstwhile business publications like *Fortune, Business Week*, and *Forbes* provide economists with a forum for reaching millions of business readers, despite the average academic economist's lack of training to address business problems. Dedicated to a technology that keeps them aloof from the everyday, they are eagerly sought after nevertheless for practical advice. Much of what economists write and say sounds trite when expressed in terms an informed person can understand. The larger public often writes critical letters to editors when economists depart from what experience and common sense suggest is true. But this is not the fault of economists. They have not been trained in public discourse. Whatever it is that academic economists do, it does not have anything to do with what businesses do. This insightful observation was made by the Nobel winner in economics, George Stigler, who said *in toto*:

> The layman . . . would find that in their professional writing the well-known columnists of *Newsweek* are quite incomprehensible. The typical article in a professional journal is unrelated to public policy – and often apparently unrelated to this world. Whether the amount of policy-advising activity of economists is rising or falling I do not know, but it is not what professional economics is about.[2]

In the economist's mind's-eye, business is a matter where decisions are made in a hypothetical marketplace populated by roboconsumers who are networked together to access all information instantaneously and programmed to reach optimum conclusions that are not unduly influenced by any individual party to the transactions. Large institutions cannot sway market decisions. Government and labor exert no special influence. Wall Street is a neutral observer. In fact, none of the growth in institutional power since the eighteenth century is of consequence.

This kind of pretentiousness would not have been tolerated by classically trained economists. In classical economics, ideas were contested by exposing them to an educated public; in addition, the keen intellects and rivalry among economists assured that puffery by a colleague would not go unpricked. Sharp criticism from within the economic fraternity was common: for example, Stanley Jevons vs David Ricardo; Joseph Schumpeter vs John Maynard Keynes; and Keynes vs Ricardo. Indeed, there is no more caustic critic of economics than one economist attacking another's theory. Keynes, for example, was devastating in his criticism of Ricardo, whose logic blocked Keynes's own innovative breakthroughs in economic thought, and who therefore needed to be discredited before Keynes's initiatives could prevail. With a biting satirical wit, Keynes attacked the unrealistic basis for his fellow economist's argument:

> [With the] . . . usual classical assumption, that there is always full employment . . . the Ricardian theory is valid, in the sense that on these suppositions there is only one rate of interest which will be compatible with full employment in the long period . . . Ricardo offers us the supreme intellectual achievement, unattainable by weaker spirits, of adopting a hypothetical world remote from experience as though it were the world of experience and then living in it consistently. With most of his successors common sense cannot help breaking in – with injury to their logical consistency.[3]

Modern economics tends to foster the use of unrealistic assumptions and, like Ricardo, to stick with them consistently. Unlike classical economics, however, no amount of evidence can contradict the current orthodoxy, because the practical consideration of whether ideas have policy relevance is itself no longer relevant.

Gerard Debreu, a professor at the University of California at Berkeley, won the Nobel prize in economics in 1983. This apparently took Debreu by surprise since his works were not widely known and his prescriptions admittedly carried no policy implications. Maurice Allais, a French professor of economics whose work is similarly complex and obscure, and who in fact was Debreu's instructor, won economics' top prize in 1988. Over the years, the Nobel committee's choices reflect an unmistakable preference for technical proficiency rather than creative thought. More accurately, the Nobel prize in economics currently recognizes achievement in mathematical logic. It would be impossible today for a conceptual genius like Joseph Schumpeter – who did not express his ideas in mathematical form – to be considered for a Nobel prize, or even, probably, to gain tenure in a top research university.

Is this the path business education wants to take? There are signs pointing in that direction. Emphasis in the highest centers of business education favor the science of research methods without reference to their usefulness. Of the major new concepts actually used by management – for example, the portfolio matrix, learning curve, strategic business unit, and matrix management – all were developed by organizations themselves or in conjunction with outside consultants.

The luxury of abstruse research in America's business schools is tolerable when management initiatives in the United States set the standards that other nations follow. However, in today's global economy the preeminence of the United States can no longer be taken for granted, and the lack of relevance in research translates into a misuse of intellectual manpower as a consequence, and potential misdirection of national and industrial policy as a real possibility.

In accounting, one of the oldest of management disciplines, a flood of publicity currently centers around the proper method for allocating overhead costs. Instead of using direct labor hours as the basic criterion, the suggestion is to shift to "activity-based accounting;" that is, looking at the factors that "drive" costs. Since capital has replaced labor as the primary "cost" in many business firms, the cost-accounting system needs to reflect this shift, as well as others, away from labor and toward true "cost-drivers." Implementation of this philosophy requires precise cost figures and reliable allocation of costs; especially in multi-product and multi-business firms. In turn, this forces development of new computer-aided systems for cost accounting.

Attention to precision in data collection in order to make better decisions is traditional accounting practice in the United States. Proposed refinements in cost-accounting data reinforce that tradition. However, the Japanese offer a new approach: looking at accounting data from the viewpoint of how they can be used to satisfy customers and motivate employees. Toshiro Hiromoto, professor of accounting at Hitotsubashi University in Tokyo, illustrates how a division of Hitachi, Japan's largest electronic and electrical company, clings to direct labor costing *because* it places an undue burden on those operations with high labor content and thus *forces* managers to automate.[4] Hitachi deliberately puts business objectives first and exactness in accounting data second. This is a basic difference in philosophy to American accounting practice, where precision is the primary objective.

An equally sharp break with American business practice is the inclination of Japanese accountants to be part of an interdisciplinary management team. Typically trained in other disciplines, the business accountant in Japan works closely with other managers in shaping consensus decisions. Professor Hiromoto uses the Daihatsu Motor Company, a medium-sized manufacturer of automobiles, to show how this works. When a new car is designed, accountants are not asked merely to supply cost estimates. Instead, Daihatsu works backward from an estimated sales price and a desired profit margin, and then approximates what costs should be. Guiding the Japanese philosophy is a belief that costs should be market driven. Market-driven management, in turn, means: "how efficiently a company *should* be able to build a product is less important than how efficiently it *must* be able to build it for maximum marketplace success."[5]

For the Japanese, accounting is simply one part of an overall organizational strategy. The strategic objective of the business is the primary "driver," and functional skills must conform to that management principle. This translates into an emphasis on nonfinancial rather than financial measures, which is contrary to American custom. The reasoning, in the Japanese mind, is simple:

If a management accounting system measures only costs, employees tend to focus on costs exclusively . . . For companies to maintain competitive advantage, employees must be continually innovative. This requires motivation . . . to improve efficiency beyond what "best practice" currently dictates. The Japanese have demonstrated that management accounting can play a significant role in integrating the innovative efforts of employees with the company's long-term strategies and goals.[6]

Results from the Japanese approach may not prove superior to Western methods. It is too early to tell. What is important, however, and opposite from conventional wisdom, is the novelty of thought it represents. A major defining difference between the United States and Japan, we have been told, is American creativity versus Japanese discipline. Yet in the examples above, it is the United States that is clinging to old technologies and the Japanese who are innovating. Japan's competitive success is in large part due to its willingness to rethink management processes instead of copying the approaches of others. It indicates Japan's pragmatic orientation to business. Once-novel Japanese practices like just-in-time inventory, quality work teams, and strong quality controls are now accepted world-wide. Not having to overcome barriers of ingrained business customs and habits allows the Japanese to conceptualize anew how businesses might best compete. A director of one of Japan's leading manufacturing companies sums it up thus:

> Theories taught in management schools are often useless when applied to practical business. That is why we think the Harvard Business School is a remarkable school but may be more of a detriment to the US economy.[7]

The distancing of theory from application is nowhere exemplified more clearly than in firm diversification. The crux of the case against diversification is the presumed inability of managers to control complex organizations effectively. If, however, managers are equal to the task of management, then nonspecialized diversification, for certain firms, holds out undeniable advantages. Just as in most sports good big players have natural advantages over good small players, good diversified companies enjoy the economies of scope *as well as scale* over comparably situated competitors who are merely big. Admittedly, excellence in managing diversity is not the hallmark of American businesses at present. Nevertheless, some companies have succeeded. And many Japanese as well as some European firms excel in this aspect of management.

The success of Japanese firms in diversifying is rooted in their attention to people. Their priority is on the individual – whether it is employees or customers. Starting with a belief that diversification is essential for growth and survival, the Japanese make workforce planning part of what they view as an inevitable process of change. Nippon Steel, for example, anticipates moving away from steel and towards electronics, engineering, urban development and services and, possibly, biotechnology. In planning this ambitious and wide-ranging changeover, Nippon Steel has developed a human resource plan that involves transferring people from steel to other fields.

The focus on incentives and motivations in attaining desired firm behavior gets relatively short shrift in theoretical models of business. To acknowledge human behavior too explicitly means dealing with uncertainty, and rigorous models in general are ill suited to deal with ambiguity. Whenever uncertainty is introduced, one runs into limits in dealing with change. When Michael Porter liberalized industry analysis within the context of the industrial economics' model, for example, he apparently felt constrained to conform strategic decision-making within relatively static industry structures and an internal rather than external view of change.

Any deterministic model robs managers of free will and, by its very construction, must treat the limiting conditions of the model as real and substantive deviations from the model as incorporeal. In explaining how and why firms diversify, this has meant ignoring the motives and actions of managements that run counter to the notion of specialization within immobilized industries.

If diversification over the long term affords a competitive advantage, American business firms will have considerable catching up to do. The cultural and structural adaptations to make diversification work would force new realities on business firms and business educators alike. It would imply an emphasis on human resource management in order to provide the glue to allow several different businesses to be managed effectively as one. At present, business seems intent on going in the opposite direction, stressing the impersonal financial aspects of management. By choosing the easier strategy of managing for short-term financial gains, rather than long-term operating improvements, American industry is conceding the advantages of diversification, if they prove to be real, to the Japanese, whose strengths in cohesive management style and people management will serve them well in extending their mastery of complex diversification at home into foreign markets; and to European companies as well, who seem more open to the possibility that nonspecialized diversification has positive economic benefits.

The ultimate decision on the merits of nonspecialized diversification will be given by the marketplace where firms compete, a proposition consistent with the dictates of theory. The marketplace, however, will not be the perfect envisionment of theorists, but, instead, a marketplace incorporating human emotions, uncertainties, and "irrational" actions: a marketplace not unlike the complex modern economy in which we live.

Notes

1 *Business Week*, 14 December 1987, p. 98.
2 George J. Stigler, *The Economist as Preacher*, (University of Chicago Press, Chicago, 1982), pp. 4–5.
3 John Maynard Keynes, *The General Theory of Employment, Interest and Money* (Harcourt Brace, New York, 1935), pp. 191–2.
4 Toshiro Hiromoto, "Another hidden edge – Japanese management accounting," *Harvard Business Review*, 66 (1988), pp. 22–6, esp. p. 23.
5 Ibid., p. 26.
6 Ibid., p. 26.
7 *Fortune*, 27 October 1986, p. 14: A quote by Asa Jonishi, director of Japan's Kyocera Corporation, the world's largest maker of ceramic packages for integrated circuits.

Index